The Millionaire Guide

For

Hair and Beauty Salons

by

NinaSkye

All information has been formulated from the mind of author unless otherwise noted and annotated. Author has the right to divulge information as per her expertise and experiences.

TABLE OF CONTENTS

Dedication

God Himself Ordered My Steps

To my Mommy, Elizabeth E. Clark, who loved me unconditionally. She gave me life, morals, ethics and God. She shaped my world allowing me to see how she was able to be superwoman, despite having six kids and a terminal illness. My life changed forever when she became my heavenly Angel guiding me through life's ups and downs and allowing her spirit to breathe through my sisters and I.

To my Daddy, LeVant M. Calhoun: My favorite man in the whole wide world. I thank you for showing me what a father looks like. I've worked hard to make you a proud papa and I love you for standing by me.

To my Sisters Bridgette, Nicky, Attyce (Rest in Paradise), Taya and Kisha: You are my lifeline. I can always count on you no matter what. I love you to the depths of my soul as we are universally connected.

To my nieces and nephews: Kendra, Desha, Donovan, Rashad, Arin, Darius, Quinci, Nicco, Kellis, Christopher, Cameron and Lennox. You can do anything you want to do in life. Never allow the world to think they need to validate you. Validate yourself. I am a proud Auntie to you all. You are truly amazing.

Also, Maxi (my "son" dog). Your unconditional love is priceless!

To my Clients and Crew: You have supported me physically, emotionally and financially. Our time in the salon and beyond is the reason you are my family. I am truly the luckiest hairstylist in the world and to say I appreciate all you do is an understatement. Thank you for staying loyal and by my side always.

To My Beautiful Wife, Sabrina Curtis You came into my life and showed me a love I have never known. Despite your apprehension of this journey, you completely showed up through this difficult process. I appreciate you even when it seems like I don't. Words can't begin to describe the way my heart beats for you. I am with you always, now and forever. I thank you for tough love, encouragement, protection and no doubt, your checkbook. I couldn't have done this without you. Your support is effervescently etched in my heart.

START INVESTING IN YOURSELF TODAY

PREFACE

Advantage for Future Millionaires

KNOW THYSELF

Today, everybody wants to be everyone but themselves. But did you know that when you are able to introduce your authentic self to the world, you're ahead of the game in winning? Why do I say this? It is because I've learned that 90 % of the people you associate with have never met themselves in a mirror. Mark Twain says it best: *"The two most Important days in your life are the day you were born and the day you find out why."* Discovering your Purpose is an advantage to your success. You are not clouded with deception of who you are because the focus is on the authentic you. Perfection is not a part of your DNA and you can accept that mistakes will be made. Now, ask yourself: *If I have the advantage in controlling the outcome of my success, what steps am I going to take to get there?*

VISION

Visionaries come in two rare forms: The Bear and the Bull which you would normally hear being used in the stock market. The thing is, it can work for entrepreneurs also. A bearish market means a suicide might happen on wall street and relates to a downtrend (losing value). A bull market means lap dances from Candy who might bring candy on wall street and relates to an uptrend (gaining value). Let's look at how these terms can be used as an entrepreneur.

As a startup, VISION should drive your goal but like a bull you're all over the place with a bomb-ass vision and very little money. You're kicking, scraping, grunting and stumbling everywhere trying to hit the fortunate target. What you're failing to see is that nine out of ten times you will get pulverized, skinned alive and used as a doormat for people to walk over. Being a bull has an upside also so let's talk about that. Ninety percent of bulls are served for lunch daily (entrepreneur graveyard) while the other ten percent, (*hmmm maybe you*) is out there not only taking hits but busting through doors creating nothing but opportunity. Bulls don't back down. They keep pounding and knocking down walls. They put up a true fight to bring their VISION alive. Some visions are clear, and some aren't but what matters is that yours will be crystal clear. It will be ready, seen, heard and accepted by millions so say to yourself: *One day my dream will become reality. Yes! It will.*

A Bull Visionary is an individual who might not be creative but sees the creativity and chooses to invest. Surprisingly, a dream is bought and paid for by a collaborated vision every day. We could categorize it by the name, venture capitalist or even worse, a loan shark. The uncharted term where taking someone else's money will claim your future money returns. I coined it bear because here you have someone gnawing, clawing, growling and breathing down your neck about your vision because they want and need their money.

Granting someone access to your dream comes with a price. For example, your bear might be your mother but wait! I'm not calling your Mom a bear but if she gave you money for your business then she would be viewed as a bear. Hibernating and waiting for that deep dent in her bank account to be refilled, making it hefty again. Now she can finally turn the room in the basement that you've been crashing in, into the red room she's wanted after reading Fifty Shades of Grey. Momma needs a life too so pay her back her money!

Now, for the sake of being real, let's hope that your bear is someone close to you and the only time the reality of the loan gets awkward is when you're face-to-face. Any other bear isn't going to hibernate any longer than the timeframe given in written terms, so it is imperative that you understand exactly what you're agreeing to. There will be no do overs because all isn't fair in business. It's all about what you negotiate. Coming face-to-face with a bear means you need leverage. Allow me to explain what I mean by this. Your vision should be solid and airtight. Staying true to your commitment is an understatement and for great reason.

First, you want to see a return on your investment and borrowing startup money puts you at the back of the line. Imagine you're entering a bull race and the announcer says take your mark while five of your competitors stand beside you (variations of bulls and bears). All six of you are ready to open your doors and the gun goes off.

The doors are jammed, and now you're out of the race. You can't compete and it's a major Setback!

A Bull or bear mentality can be great with the right visionaries considered. Always play to your strengths and a strong advisory board.

HATERS

All great success stories started with a good ole' fashion hater. From the beginning of time hate has been used to bring success to the ones it was inflicted upon. Look what hate did for Pharaoh. We know his name and his legends. Now look at Legends of God, her wrath and out of all creation has the most sold book today existing "The Holy Bible"

Here is a list of some of my favorite Rivals. Good, Bad or indifferent we know the legend of all.

- Nicholas Tesla vs Thomas Edison.
- Elmer Fudd vs Bugs Bunny
- Professor X vs Magneto
- Lace Fronts vs Natural Hair
- Butter vs Margarine
- Biggie vs Tupac
- 50 Cent vs Mayweather
- Redskins vs Dallas Cowboys
- Superman vs Batman (Yes, Bruce Wayne is a Hater)
- Day vs Night
- Steve Jobs vs Bill Gates
- Opioids vs Cannabis
- The New England Patriots vs Every other team in the NFL

(last but not least)

- My Mac & Cheese vs My Sisters

I hope you get what I'm saying here. Although I'm not a big fan of hate, I use it to conquer my opponent in a *Game of Thrones* dead versus living kind of way. You must plan for a sneak attack! Be different, patient, disciplined, fearless, humble and most of all, hungry. You must have the appetite of the Bull and Bear paired with the Eye of the Tiger. This deadly combination will drive your soul to thrive on pure instinct. Mastering the skill to rely on instincts is some next-level knowledge that only a few are crazy enough to tap into. Being motivated by hate is a true force that will help mold and shape your dream into a tangible reality.

KNOWLEDGE

If you've heard it once, you've heard a million times: Knowledge is Power! Queen Cersei herself demonstrated it best in an episode of *Game of Thrones*. However, it is something to be said in knowing, understanding, and grasping the mere comprehension of realizing that power is power. It is contradictory because not everyone possesses this knowledge.

FAILURE

If you're afraid to put yourself out there, you are among 90% who feel the same. *Shocked, huh?* See when you do what 90% does, you have no drive to follow your dreams. The fear of success impels you to do nothing and that is why 90% of the population are employees not bosses. Only bosses conquer fear in the workplace. I don't know about you, but I feel like a caged animal chained to a clock who must ask permission to do basic non-boss stuff like clock out. After being self-employed for over fifteen years I was forced to do something I wasn't prepared to do. I had to go back to work for a corporation. This move wasn't part of my original game plan but only God himself could orchestrate such a flawed masterpiece such as myself. When all else fails, you learn that God is your only source and if you've never failed, you haven't reached your full potential. Just like pain failure is your ally. Failure teaches you the true meaning of success and without it, we gain no leverage in survival.

The world we live in it is perfectly imperfect. If you don't win you lose and the only way to win is to fail. From the time you were born, this was a learned behavior. You didn't come out walking and falling was inevitable. Some babies scraped a knee, fell and hit their head, and even cried so that someone would pick them up. But when all else failed, they got back up and didn't give up. Failure is our best antidote for success. Embrace it!

CHAPTER 1

TODAY IS A NEW DAY

A CHANGED LIFE

On this day you are being held accountable for your success! Write this date down in your calendar or glue it to your vision board and keep in mind that this is a date to be remembered.

Once you recognize that success is different for everyone, it will help you understand that it is no hidden jewel. Success will reveal just who YOU really are!

YOU GOT THIS!

Are you attempting to make money or is making a difference more significant? Being honest with yourself always yields the best results.

I learned that the hard way. Believing my own deception was an attempt to lead others to believe what I believed was true. I realized very quickly that you can deceive everyone else, but you can't deceive yourself. *A perfect example would be:* To tell yourself *I'm stupid* and

believe it, others would believe you're stupid also . I digress. It's time to appreciate the knowledge you will receive along this journey to achieving success. Change your habits, change your life.

START HERE

Now that the hardest part is over, it's time to get started. Starting is not as difficult as accepting that change is needed but it can be a difficult task. Starting means the awakening of a mindset. An unfamiliar type of mindset like, *I've had enough of not changing how I do things mindset*. Today, we will start by making a promise to change. By doing so, you can expect to see the evolution from your change. The great thing about change is that it has no rules, no time restraints and it isn't governed by laws. Change is inevitable and indestructible. Change is a true rebel elevated to its highest edge like a gliding pair of

"Sam Villa" shears cutting its way through silky long hair at the salon and getting that exact precise blunt style. Change is intense heat and pressure that creates the diamond you are! Change is all you need to make that life-changing decision. Change is good (sista waving hair) *Amen!*

If   done   right   you   only   have   to   enter   here   once

Here is where you dig deep, deep into that graveyard of skeleton bones, grab your shovel and begin digging up all the lies you've ever told yourself. "No one has to know except me of course".

Now say! OMG… I knew you were lying, *Ha Ha! Oh! Well I didn't believe you anyway.*

Great….woooh! Glad we got that out of the way.

Huh!! Oh, my bad, you're not done yet. Sure, I'll wait.

NEW YOU!

Hey there pretty woman. Oh My! Look at you, shining bright like a diamond. You look great from head to toe, *hmmm hmmm*. Ok, let's get back to business.

REALITY

We all need a reality check every now and then. Not the one you typically think of but one that goes a bit deeper. This reality check speaks to whether you have it or not. If you don't have it, then it's time to go get it. It's okay to get out there and earn your stripes. No need to whine about it because the passion and determination is there. You just need to believe it and keep moving. This is the time to come up with that non-negotiable list of making your dreams come true. Author and leadership guru John C. Maxwell have what he calls the *Dream Test*. This test is for BIG dreamers who set out to achieve their dream. Are you ready to step into the reality of what a million dollar look like? If you said Yes, dig deep and answer John's top ten questions.

1. Is my dream really my dream? If it's really yours, Own it!
2. Do I clearly see my dream? Be vivid. Allow your imagination to create vibrant images of what your dream looks like. Be as specific as you can.
3. Am I depending on things within my control? Be realistic. Are you asking for things you're not working towards? For example: Becoming a millionaire requires action behind the intent and you're taking a step in the right direction reading this book.
4. Do I have the energy to achieve it? This is all about passion. Will you follow through or just quit when the going gets tough because it will?
5. Do I have a strategy? This one thing can annihilate your intentions so planning and strategizing is something you must get used to.
6. Who do I have around me that can help me? Use your resources and don't be prideful. Ask for help because you're powerless as one and it can kill any business. You will be stressed enough so use all the help you can get.

7. Am I willing to pay the price? Are you all in?
8. Does working towards my dream bring satisfaction? You must grow and develop yourself in pursuit of your dream. If there's no satisfaction in making your dream come true, then maybe this isn't the dream you should chase.
9. Are you moving closer? Pure tenacity! Are you closer today than you were yesterday?
10. Does my dream benefit others? If you are doing this solely for you something is bound to go wrong. In any busy the more people you can connect with the more money you will make.

http://www.littlethingsmatter.com/blog/2011/01/27/put-your-dream-to-the-test-by-dr-john-maxwell/

Believing you have something to offer should be 100% authentic. Nothing fake should even cross your mind. Whatever you're selling should be something your client wants to buy. Is it good? Does it feel great? Does it tell a story? Does it add value, peace, happiness or any type of emotional fulfillment? Is it going to be the best experience of their life and is it going to make a difference?

You must answer all these questions and more. Consumers are becoming very selective on where they spend their money.

CHAPTER 2

TRUTH HURTS

I can recall a time when people would buy things just because they liked or loved it and wanted it, period. It could have been that they were simply trying to keep up with the Joneses but. None of that matters. What does matter is that the world wants to know you and what you stand for. A world that defines your character by standing or kneeling doesn't know you at all. You must get to a place of voicing your truth authentically and unapologetically.

Now it's time to reflect and spend some time with You! Have that conversation with yourself to confirm that you definitely have what it takes to have the mindset of a millionaire. Hope you're with me because I know I'm *Damn Right!* **Your truth may hurt a bit,** but it will not leave a scar if you're willing to examine your truth for what it is.

Ready to discover where you are emotionally when it comes to becoming an entrepreneur? There are three types of entrepreneurs:

1. **The WannaBe**

2. **The TrynaBe**
3. **The BabyBe**

An example of the WannaBe is one that we can all relate to. "The Rip-off Kitchen Stylist".

I'm not talking about the traditional *come to my basement and I'll cut, color and relax your hair for $30.00 stylist*. I'm talking about the *no license, no hair school training, using regular beauty supply products, charging half down deposits on social media stylist*. They pay no taxes and charge professional prices. If this is you or someone you know, going back to school is a crucial step to being successful in your business. The money will still be there but you're going about building your business the right way. Malpractice suits are real and so is incarceration. Stop, hijacking a profession calling it a business.

An example of the TrynaBe shouldn't come as a surprise either because this person is trying to fit into them all without the appropriate credentials.

A makeup artist at MAC, a skin therapist, and a hair stylist. I'm not saying that a person cannot have many skills but when one is trying to do all these things without gaining the proper training, education and/or credentials, it lacks focus.

Focus is extremely important and becomes a powerful tool that many will never learn to master. I know that's not you, right?

You can't be a jack of all trades and a master of none. ~unknown

Equip yourself by sharpening your armor (your strengths), not by counseling your failures (attempting to work through your weaknesses). In business, the weak is barred from all parties. Early morning meetings or trolling through the kitchen for midnight cake, *oops!* I meant snack.

I must admit that I lost that battle way too often. However, try to be better, smarter, faster, obedient, still, clear, humble, blessed, at peace, focused, driven, passionate, giving, accepting, inspiring, determined, loving, genuine, different, rare, pure, grateful, strategic, meticulous, bold, edgy, and rocker. In other words, BE rebellious to change to the best version of You!

An example of the BabyBe, my friend, is where it counts. Around this time your perspective starts to shift. You've adjusted from a consumer mindset to a producer's mindset.

Con.sum.er – a person who purchases goods and services for personal use.

Pro.du.cer - viewing the world from the opposite side of the lens. You're looking to create.

Debt is not your friend at this stage. If you're a WannaBe or TrynaBe, you're not too late to jump on board of being debt free. As a BabyBe, debt consumes your life (con.su.mer). When your debt pile is bigger than your bank account your focus is not on the right thing.

Before I became focused on my business, I didn't think my debt mattered. I thought I could do it all despite owing my creditors, but the truth is I was amazed at how this forced accountability in my face and just like I had to be accountable, I'm asking you to hold yourself accountable. No one is perfect but you must work on it to get the job done. Take ownership in all things and the blessing to build a deep relationship with yourself will be manifested. Remember, your voice matters and truthfully, only your voice matters. Advice is certainly welcomed but, in your business, you must call the shots. This is non-negotiable. The decision must be 100% yours.

Everything Rises and Falls on Leadership

What does this mean? Everything starts and ends with you. Someone very wise told me: *"You are the example. Be the example and Lead by example."* Doing this will help you in your decision making. Play out different scenarios through a process of elimination and deductive reasoning. *For example:* Play out a multitude of different scenarios and determine your answers from a logical point of view. The longer you avoid this process the more likely your end game will get a new move-in date.

Being a decisive decision maker doesn't always mean it's the right decision or the best decision. It means that even if you fail, you take accountability and move on. You're not living with a should have, could have, or would have mentality. You're not blaming your team, or anyone else. Everything rises and falls on you.

CHAPTER 3

DECISIONS, DECISIONS, DECISIONS

If your vision is evolving, you're learning and that's a good thing. You're not afraid of change and can see nothing but the best in yourself even if that means confronting your fears. Seriously, when have you ever tried to not be scared? When was the last time you knew you feared something, closed your eyes (pic calm with eyes closed) and thought to yourself, *don't be scared* and *Bloop!* You opened your eyes all excited and the fear was gone? Never, right?

Prayer may work in the moment as comfort, but fear is still there. Stare fear in the face and know that if God sends you to it, He will see you through it. Welcome fear even if it's frightening or unknown.

Fear may look like Freddy Krueger, Jason, or Mike Myers on a play date with Pumpkin head trying to drag you through a Pet Cemetery at 11:14pm while a Psycho chases you down Route 66 trying to escape 13 Ghost running towards The House on Haunted Hill, while Von Miller, Khalil Mack and J.J. Watt are screaming GET OUT!

Wow! Now that sounds like a whole lot of scary, huh? (describing this scene).

I mentioned this to prove a point. One word: *Survival*. Life can sometimes throw some scary, unpredictable circumstances your way but to be a leader you must be ready to welcome fear. It will lead you to your greatest victories or unwarranted defeats. Your growth starts there. It's like yin and yang all day. If you're afraid of deciding, guess what? You still must make it. In addition to that, if you make the wrong decision, it was still the right decision because you now know what not to do. This will direct your energy to doing what you know is right. Of course, that implies to understanding and listening to yourself or perhaps, the Holy Spirit (the inner voice we all have). The problem here is that we love to play victim, so we procrastinate and/or stay in a bad situation far too long. Leading is not always glory. It's pure inspiration. It's the courage to shape the minds of others and yourself, aspiring to reach greatness. It's also how cults are born, so be careful and understand that who you follow determines who you lead. Everything rises and falls on you. Pointing blame is never allowed.

Are you A Leader?

Some say leaders are born. Some say leaders are molded. Throughout history leaders have forged new paths for others to follow. Sometimes a leader might fail but they grow from experiences and become stronger like our history has proven with Madam C.J. Walker, Oprah Winfrey, and Beyonce Knowles. Three stars aren't enough!

Challenges aren't roadblocks to leaders; they are opportunities. Leaders do not make excuses because their focus is more on succeeding and making a difference in the lives of others.

Fact: 88% of entrepreneurs come from extremely rich families.

Leaders are not limited to the old and experienced. A leader's performance is measured by the people who follow them, how they inspire them, and how they engage them.

Leadership Quotes

"Management is doing everything right; leadership is doing the right things." ~Peter F. Drucker

"A leader is one who knows the way, goes the way, and shows the way." ~John C. Maxwell

"Innovation distinguishes between a leader and a follower." ~Steve Jobs

"If your actions inspire others to dream more, learn more, do more and become more, you are a leader." ~John Quincy Adams

"Leaders must be close enough to relate to others, but far enough ahead to motivate them." ~John C. Maxwell

Leaders are: Visionaries, Educators, Innovators, Motivators, Communicators, Facilitators, and Advisors

https://www.youtube.com/watch?v=6U53QTun-w

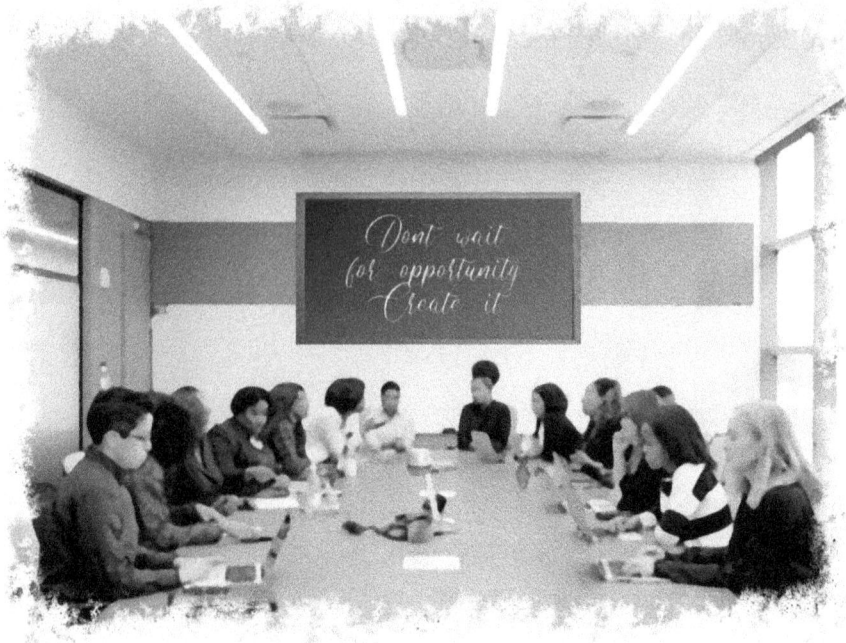

CHAPTER 4
UNDERESTIMATION

The Power of Being Underestimated

First rule: underestimate no one. While they may underestimate you, it has become a classic truth that your haters should be your motivators. It's very good fuel to ignite that fire in you! You can sit and be bitter or decide to bounce back stronger than ever. We've all seen the Karate Kid with Ralph Macchio and the new Karate Kid with Jaden Smith for the millennials. One moved to a foreign place and the other moved to a foreign country. They were uncomfortable, unsure, lonely then bullied.

They had to learn a new city, a new school and then they had to learn karate. They were laughed at, counted out and at one point, injured. But even after their opponent cheated to win, they still walked away winners.

Brace yourself and expect to be uncomfortable! At times you will be unsure and lonely. It will be necessary for you to learn new things, maybe perhaps go back to school and still walk away a winner. Become the Karate Kid. While their opponents were laughing and counting them out, they were preparing for a war that they endured and came out on top.

"One of the best opportunities you can be given in life is to be underestimated." -unknown

WannaBe's and TrynaBe's are showboats. They show you everything they're doing because they can't keep their mouths shut. This piece of advice I give to you to carry as your secret weapon. Listen to everything they say and observe everything they do. See what their weaknesses are and find a way to capitalize on it. Become a problem solver and learn to create solutions. Stop committing industry incest by doing what you see other stylist doing. Stop copying and pasting other people routines, claiming them as your own. Stay out of drama and gossip and view situations from a producer's mindset. Ask yourself: *Is there an opportunity here?* If not, keep it moving. Millionaires have no time for nonsense because they're too busy finding creative ways to get rewarded.

Why should I do business with you instead of loudmouth Billy Jean?

You never want clients or customers asking why your prices are higher. The overall service should justify your prices. If it doesn't, you're considered a rip off. All fees should be charged accordingly. Some of the worst stylist are the most expensive and every client isn't paying for skill. They pay for so much more like ambiance, fresh flowers in the bathroom, perhaps a personalized locker and robe. Know what lane you're in and switch lanes appropriately. Do I plan to stay? I think not! Eventually my haters will witness my rewards.

Your competition is your homework. The assignment is their customer's complaints. View the world from a producer's mindset. Allow that to sink in.

Produce – A person or company that manufacture from raw materials. Bring into existence.

Make sure you are offering great customer service and using awesome products. These two things alone will increase your revenue.

Want to look back and see the growth in your business? Invest in your business name, logo, slogan, advertising and marketing. Invest in how you want to incorporate your business.

Start building in silence and move beyond the shadows always. Go to places where your opposition isn't welcomed. Uncharted territory where only the brave survives. This is where you dwell day in and day out. Your vision must become your reality. Surface thinking won't cut it. You must deconstruct everything you see and know and reconstruct it with everything you've learned. Rebuilding by scratch allows you the opportunity to construct a strong foundation with no cracks.

If it isn't perfect, you understand what needs work. The more you do this the clearer your vision becomes. Move simultaneously and strategically and try not to let time pass or people will forget you exist. In some cases, this works in your favor if you're moving behind the scenes. If you're watching Netflix and chilling every day of the week, a reality check is needed. ASAP! You want *"the others"* to assume you're no threat while you're in the books, classrooms, webinars, summits and training on a consistent basis. Sharpening your shears, shining your armor, polishing your shoes and fixing your crown. You're not going to look ready like a WannaBe or act ready like a TrynaBe. You're going to be ready because you're a BabyBe that learned from the IllionillyBe's (keep reading to understand the meaning of this word).

As of 2015, I have heard whispers that the day of a physical salon is dead. It isn't impossible; however, it needs to be well executed. For years salons slid under the radar because there was no proof in how much profit was made. They laughed and made comments like *"oh she just does hair."* So, we had to become loud and wear our money being flashy with our shoes, bags, cars and houses.

After people noticed us, became friends with us, and observed us they realized they could capitalize on us.

We sacrificed our body, creativeness and time while they are watching Netflix and chilling, perhaps traveling to see the 8th Wonder of the World, all because we failed to see the opportunities in ourselves. Well, not anymore. We must learn from our mistakes and other people's mistakes. Don't wait until tomorrow when you can start today. Think about what success looks like for you.

Successful entrepreneurs are what I call the IllionillyBe's. They acknowledge that there must be a method to your madness. Let your ideas manifest, go through multiple scenarios, shape them, mold them and sculpt them to create your vision. Share this vision with the right people because most won't understand. Some will even tell you that you're crazy. The good news is that You Are! Only crazy people are courageous enough to start a real business based on a dream and born from an idea destined for reality.

Take time to discover your non-negotiables. Knowing the foundation you're standing on will solidify your strengths and expose your weaknesses (to yourself). Here is where you focus solely on your strengths. IllionillyBe's do what they are absolutely great in. They are risk takers, playmakers, negotiators, hell raisers, trailblazers, educators, inspirators, innovators, decision makers, and most definitely money makers.

Business Leaders Quotes

Reference: Employersresource.com

Herb Kelleher – Southwest Airlines

"You must be very patient and very persistent. The world isn't going to shower gold coins on you just because you have a good idea. You're going to have to work like crazy to bring that idea to the attention of people. They're not going to buy it unless they know about it."

"Power should be reserved for weightlifting and boats, and leadership really involves responsibility."

Your employees come first. And if you treat your employees right, guess what? Your customers come back, and that makes your shareholders happy. Start with employees and the rest follows from that."

Leading by example will create awesome leaders.

Warren Buffet – Berkshire Hathaway

"It takes 20 years to build a reputation and five minutes to ruin it. If you think about that you'll do things differently."

Imagine where you are today. If you're in a place where you must rebrand, starting now is your only option. This isn't a race to the finish line. Be strategic on how you position yourself. Construct your vision to work and train with people that can propel you faster.

This is where you show up, assist, help and be a reliable person they can depend on. How you network is extremely important. #figureitout. There are only 24-hours in a day, so maximize every hour.

I'm sitting at work, waiting on a late client, listening to music (it motivates me) while writing this book. At home I watch tv (mainly during football season) - *hail to the redskins.* I read two books simultaneously. One in my hand and the other on my phone. In deep thought: *write my book, take notes and research everything.* On other days I turn everything off and focus on one thing. I learn what I need to learn and I do whatever I need to do including going to sleep at 4:00am to greet my client at 10:00am. When my wife comes home after working two jobs and tells me about her day, time is never an excuse. I still make sure she eats and feed Maxi (our dog/son) before she dozes off. #figureitout

Warren Buffet – Berkshire Hathaway

"The most important thing to do if you find yourself in a hole is to stop digging."

"I insist on a lot of time being spent, almost every day, to just sit and think. That is very uncommon in American business! I read and think. So I do more reading and thinking, and make less impulse decisions than most people in business. I do it because I like this kind of life".

If you read his quotes and think *what more Warren Buffet needs to learn*, you're missing the point. He chooses to learn because there is more to learn to help him grow. I believe that helps him to be more effective, introduces him to new technology, new customers or simply a better way of execution.

We as human beings have a way of trying to make a square fit into a rectangle. Yes, it may fit but is it necessary? Does it look right? Does it take up space instead of maximizing its full potential? Every square inch of the rectangle matters just like your salon/studio. Construct it in a way that the functionality makes sense. Challenge the status quo. If you're content with thinking like everyone else, you're not really thinking.

Satya Nadella- Microsoft

"Longevity in this business is about being able to reinvent yourself or invent the future."

Think back to the first Pepsi you ever drank. Does it look the same? No, it doesn't! Not because Pepsi wasn't making money. They knew that to stay relevant they had to be an innovator. Pepsi isn't just a soda. It is a brand and a way of life for some.

We live in a society where posting the wrong video becomes right. Individuals are going from being inspired by Nicki Minaj to beefing with her in a matter of a new signed record deal. Seriously, do you think Cardi B had that on her bucket list *hmmmm ...create a beef with Nicki Minaj, check.* Of course not!

Reality TV is producing millionaires and *I say this in the most honest way.* It isn't because there's something so magnificent about them. It's because they see the monetary value in it. What matters is the audience that is willing to watch these shows, listen to them, follow them on social media and pay extra for the cable networks. People have become big business and it's not based on talent. It's based on sales. Remember when Sprite went hip-hop? Not because Tupac, Biggie and Jay-Z are their top favorite artists but because they have access to gain potential customers.

Reed Hastings – Netflix

"I'm invested Are You?"

"Most entrepreneurial ideas will sound crazy, stupid and uneconomic, and then they'll turn out to be right."

The thing is, they still exist.

Think about how many years it has been since the world was lit by kerosene lamps. Now we have an abundance of electricity. When was the last time Jack and Jill went up a hill to fetch a pail of water?

These people had a dream that became a vision that was executed even though they were called crazy or stupid. I prefer to call them brilliant. I remind myself often that it's okay for others not to believe in my vision because that is for me to do. #figureitout

Henry (Hot Damn!) Ford – Founder of Ford Motor Company

"If you think you can do a thing or think you can't do a thing, you're right."

"Coming together is a beginning, staying together is progress and working together is success."

You were born into sin and given free will. You have the power to set limits on that will. #period

When everything seems to be going against you, remember that the airplane takes off against the wind, not with it.

This goes back to embracing fear so Don't EVER allow it to take over in any area of your life! Brace for impact. You can obliterate your opposition if you go full speed ahead. Of course, you should use caution and realize the upside. Do not crash into the land of a downside risk.

Wow! I'm surprised to discover that I am a history enthusiast because I love wise people and I aspire to be one.

My point is that many like myself believe that on April 15th, 1912 the RMS Titanic wouldn't have sunk if it had just hit the iceberg head on.

The fatal mistake besides not having binoculars, an arrogant owner and potential insurance scam (allegedly) was trying to miss the iceberg. By turning that big hunk of steel, exposing the more vulnerable side, opening her right up by a grazing swipe. Fact.

Had the Titanic gone forward, *Yes! In this case*, the people could have held on and buckled down. They could have chosen to embrace the impact since it was unavoidable. If only they had known, so many lives wouldn't have been lost, including Jack.

So, how does this information help me? Building a failing business will lead you and your team to the same fate. Traveling in the dark of uncharted waters with no binoculars and crashing into something you didn't see coming. The only question that is left for you to answer is: will you be like the owner of the Titanic and abandon ship or will you go down with it?

Being afraid of the inevitable means you're going to get side swiped and take a whole lot of people with you. Especially in business.

As I mentioned earlier: Everything rises and falls with you! Check your emotions at the door and know that they do not have a place to live when it comes to your business.

Henry Ford – Ford Motor Company

"Quality means doing everything right when no one is looking."

FOCUS

Don't make it a hobby to be a jack of trades but a master of none. FOCUS solely on your strengths and learn from your weaknesses. In the life of Google and YouTube, you can build a full functioning business. Stimulate your brain with research or it will starve from lack of knowledge. The more you learn the more you want to learn. It becomes a way of life because your mindset is engraved with learning more and more.

Knowledge has a way of motivating change and let me explain why. The brain has no true filtering process. Typically, once you've heard or seen something you can never unhear or un-see. It is either lying and waiting in your conscience or lying dormant in your sub-conscience. No matter which one it is, it's always there. *For example:* Your mindset before reading this book could remain the same. You may choose to not utilize the strategies in this book, but you could never un-read it. Knowledge is power whether you use it or not.

Warren Buffet – Berkshire Hathaway

"Anyone who stops learning is old, whether at 20 or 80. Anyone who keeps learning stays young. The greatest thing in life is to keep your mind young."

QUICK, DON'T BLINK!

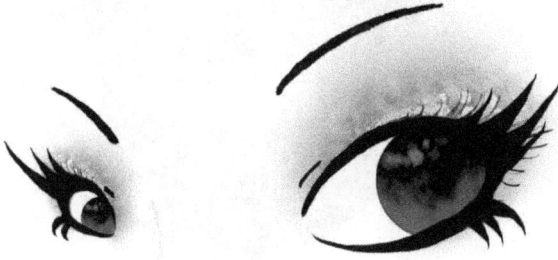

Learn, read, observe, study, research, engage and listen. Feed your brain. It is a muscle. Without nutrition it will starve and die. #period

"If everyone is moving forward together, then success should take care of itself." ~Me

Build warriors, leaders and thinkers. Just like we construct buildings we can construct the minds that are in them. We need to change when it comes to educating and evolving as a person.

Quote Alley exists because it's instant inspiration and motivation. It's meant to become part of your daily existence.

This book will give you plenty of references, however, consider it as my early Christmas gift to you.

CHAPTER 5

(N.U.A.) NEVER UNDERESTIMATE ANYONE

MJ Demarco – Author of the Millionaire Fastlane

"You're having problems finding success because you're on an everlasting search for a shortcut."

Shortcuts do not exist. JUST DO THE WORK!

The Millionaire Fastlane is a book you need to pick up. As a matter of fact, I would recommend it to be your next read. It teaches the importance of:

- Need
- Entry
- Scale
- Control
- Time

N.E.S.C.T. (Next)

The Commandment of Need (N)

Stop chasing money and chase needs. Find a problem and create a solution.

What services or products can use a face lift in the beauty industry? How can you implement technology to make your work more efficient? Stop focusing on what makes you happy unless you want to be your only customer. Listen and observe everything around you and eventually your producer mindset will be awakened.

The Commandment of Entry (E)

"If getting into business is as simple as paying 200.00 for a distributor kit, there are no entry barriers and the opportunity should be passed by. If anyone can sign up and start your business what's so spectacular about that?" In so many words, try as hard as possible to avoid rush hour traffic, it puts you in direct line with your competition. Your strategy on how you connect with your target audience is important. You must travel a different road, use new methods and create a smooth landing for your arrival. Move in a way that you don't have to chase customers and customers will chase you.

The Commandment of Scale (S)

Building a scalable business means to maintain or improve profit margins while increasing sales volume at a rapid rate. Being able to cut cost and meet product/service demand must be perfectly executed. Trying to scale your business without the right resources and manpower can kill your business.

I remember on Shark Tank a business by the name "Daisy Cakes" appeared on an episode and made a deal with Barbara Corcoran. On the night it aired her website crashed and she couldn't complete a significant amount of orders. The deal became her worst nightmare. She went from excitement to drowning in her tears, all in a matter of hours. Simply, because she didn't have systems in place to meet the demand. Although she wanted to accommodate the order requests, she didn't realize how the world would gravitate to her site after hearing her story on the Shark Tank. The good news is that she has a Shark on her team and today, "Daisy Cakes" has done over 5 million dollars in sales.

The Commandment of Control (C)

This is a tricky one for stylists because we are in the service business. We hate to admit it, but we don't have control over our business; our clients do. How about the salon you work in or for? What will you do tomorrow or next week if all your clients cancel or an *Under New Management* sign is on the door when you arrive to work? If an algorithm changes on social media, Shopify, eBay or Amazon, what will be your next move? Your goal in business is to create something you can control. Some of you reading this book have thousands of followers on Instagram not realizing how Facebook developers are discussing the relevance of taking away likes on your pages and reworking how people interact with you. Are you prepared for this? If that Y2K comes back around, will you lose all your contacts? If so, you have work to do. Saving your contacts to more than one Gmail account, uploading them to your computer or purchasing a rolodex are things you can control now.

The Commandment of Time (T)

Time is so undervalued by most human beings. It makes us such a walking contradiction. Saying phrases like "time waits for no man", "time isn't on your side" and "time is running out" but still living as if we have all the time in the world to make our dreams come true. Millionaires realize time is priceless. It is one thing you can't get back. Chasing millionaire status will require you to be extremely selfish with your time. Prioritize your schedule so you can create more time to focus on growing your business now instead of putting it off until tomorrow. A lot can change between now and then.

CHAPTER 6

GOLDEN KEY

Millionaire Mindset

It is my "soul" purpose to prepare you for the road that lies ahead. Us as "artists" are too consumed with our artistic works that we leave our business for someone else to mind and in some cases your "business" can become completely rogue. It can also be a dangerous decision. Always have an exit strategy. Your end-game strategy is just as important as the begin-game strategy.

Work Smarter not Harder

I want you to know that I get it! Working at a commission salon for the purpose of gaining clients to earn a steady income is easier, *Huh?* Well, perhaps it can be. However, because your employer covers your operating, product, financial, legal, health, etc., they reap all the rewards and give you what they say you're worth. Your worth and gift is invaluable and giving others permission to pay you what they want diminishes everything that you're working for.

Even when no one else bets on you, you must bet on yourself. In Vegas there is one simple reason the house always wins. You're playing by their rules.

Key 1

Per *POTUS (President of the United States)*

Try borrowing 1,000,000 from your parents. (crazy laughing looks). This strategy is for those who probably didn't buy this book.

Key 2

If you are fortunate enough to have capital but are stagnant and losing profits year after year then you have management issues.

If you have no management team then hire one and if you do have a management team then fire them and hire a new one.

I know it sounds harsh, but it is facts. Everything rises and falls with you.

You are the visionary. Your business needs your complete focus on being an innovator. Your management team should be your driving force. As a start-up or small business, I know money can be tight, but you must have a team to help grow your business.

Interns, mentors, students of the trade and college students are extremely eager and affordable. In a sustainable and profitable business that you are trying to scale, your team should look something like this:

- Visionary – You of course, although it could be *someone else.*
- Operational Manager – Oversee the day-to-day operations. Hiring employees, inventory, deliveries, paper, etc.

- Finance – Responsible for the business financial health, investment strategies, long-term financial goals, etc.
- Expansion – Helps develop your shop network, handles location analysis, etc.
- Marketing Manager – Absolutely necessary in every business even if you're a behind-the-chair stylist. Coordinating marketing strategies and sales activities should be done consistently.
- Legal – An Attorney should always be close by. Most contracts are written in favor of the other party meaning not you so, always have legal counsel.
- Sales Team – Your Soldiers and they should be a force to be reckoned with.
- Business Development – For expansion and to diversify amongst industries.

These areas should be carefully researched. We have a mentorship program for you to join if you need assistance.

One million dollars isn't difficult to achieve at all. It's a simple mathematical equation.

If you're a salon owner with ten employees, don't delegate; participate. At least one out of your ten employees have a vision, If you're fortunate, maybe two of them will make up your new team. Genuinely talk to them and find out what they are passionate about. Take the time to see how you can be of help. Business is always about elevating others into their greatness, especially when those that you help are ones that contributed to your success.

All beauty professionals with clientele should set high expectations when looking for a salon home. Stop settling for whatever comes your way. The ideal salon invests in their team and re-invest in their clients. Choosing to build together is always the better option, so get to know your crew.

Investment Club

I absolutely love this idea.

Starting an investment club (with people you trust), can be the best idea ever, especially if you can do this with family and friends. Research and trust are mandatory when it comes to putting coins on the table, however, you must find the best strategies.

Learning about the stock market can be a challenging move but just like everything else, once you get it, you've got it. For years you have heard that it's easy to lose money in the stock market and risky. That all might be true but isn't that life. One minute you're up the next minute your down. Sit back and look in your closet or outside your window and think about how much your clothes, shoes and car depreciated in value, *hmmmm.* You still brought them, and none will pay you interest or compound interest.

A client of mine started investing at the age of 23. She was taught by an older gentleman that she worked with. As a black woman she was terrified from hearing negative comments about how she would lose money but fortunately for her, she faced her fear. At 42, she was set. She couldn't believe how her money had grown. In, 2008 when Bernie Madoff caused financial chaos, she told me she had lost a lot of money. I'm talking about 100k in loss. What stood out to me was the fact she had 100k to lose and what she would say next is the reason why a stock portfolio is a good investment.

The government was in a shutdown crisis. Worse than the one we're in as I write this book but, just like that, Obama signed an executive order to bail them out. Major companies like JP Morgan and General Motors were facing a catastrophe that would trickle down to the American people losing their jobs, homes, cars and financial security (some did by the way). Bernie Madoff's son even hung himself on the day of his arrest anniversary. Tragic.

The economy and Wall Street were saved because of that bailout and so was my client. She had made her money back and more. It hadn't taken a decade either. No savings account is going to grow your coins the way the market does. I asked her if there was anything she regrets when investing and she said yes. I should have taken more risks. *Wow*, I thought.

Perspective after an experience should always shift your mindset. Going in, she was afraid she would lose money. Afterwards, she witnessed the money she lost. The younger you are, the more calculated risk you should be willing to take.

One of my millionaire clients lived on 25% of her income. She saved and invested the other 75%. She had a positive mindset on what money can really do for you. I always say *money might not grow on trees however, it does grow.* Another thing my client does is pay her 9 and 10-year old sons three dollars a week for chores and when they get to $30, she only allows them to spend half. The other half is invested. Amazing, huh? I thought the same.

I've heard stories of other investors only supporting companies where they are shareholders. For example: They wear Nike, drink Coca Cola, sport yoga pants from Walmart, shop on Amazon and all their bling comes from Tiffany's. Clever, right? I thought so too.

On average, a cosmetologist spends ten to fifteen dollars a day on food and snacks, an estimated $450.00 a month. Some of us spend more. *Hello!* So, let's say approximately $500.00 a month on lunch and snacks, totaling $6000.00 a year. This could be a potential investment by eliminating this one money wasting habit and could grow your bank account to $60,000 in ten years. However, if you want your money to grow by investing, take a close look at the chart below growing at a rate as high as 9%.

15 Years of investing $500.00

https://www.investor.gov/additional-resources/free-financial-planning-tools/compound-interest-calculator

Total Savings

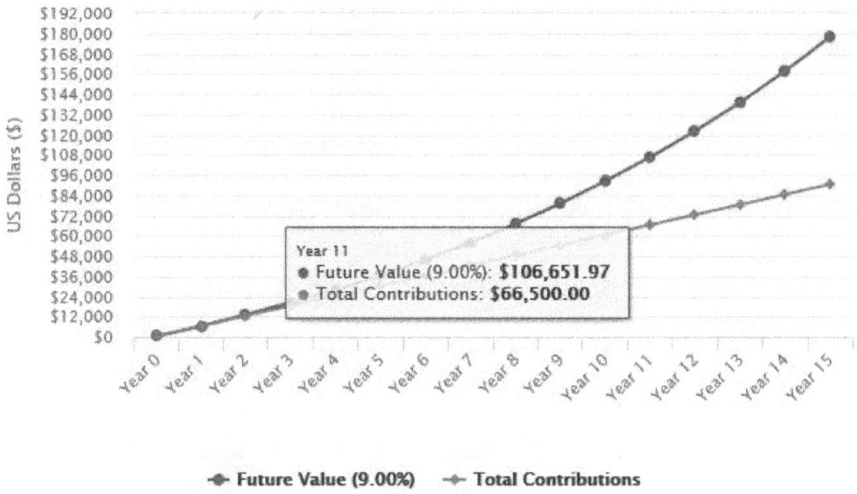

Chart showing Total Savings with Future Value (9.00%) and Total Contributions from Year 0 to Year 15.

Year 11
- Future Value (9.00%): **$106,651.97**
- Total Contributions: **$66,500.00**

Legend: Future Value (9.00%) — Total Contributions

Investor.gov

Years	Future Value (9.00%)	Total Contributions
Year 0	$500.00	$500.00
Year 1	$6,545.00	$6,500.00
Year 2	$13,134.05	$12,500.00
Year 3	$20,316.11	$18,500.00
Year 4	$28,144.56	$24,500.00
Year 5	$36,677.58	$30,500.00
Year 6	$45,978.56	$36,500.00
Year 7	$56,116.63	$42,500.00
Year 8	$67,167.12	$48,500.00
Year 9	$79,212.17	$54,500.00
Year 10	$92,341.26	$60,500.00

Year 11	$106,651.97	$66,500.00
Year 12	$122,250.65	$72,500.00
Year 13	$139,253.21	$78,500.00
Year 14	$157,786.00	$84,500.00
Year 15	$177,986.74	$90,500.00

15 Years

https://www.investor.gov/additional-resources/free-financial-planning-tools/compound-interest-calculator

20 Years

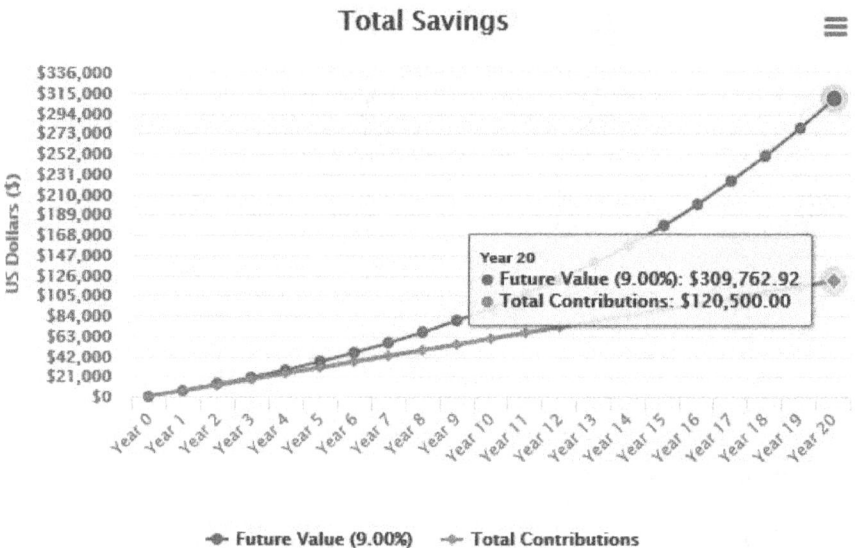

Total Savings

Year 20
● Future Value (9.00%): $309,762.92
● Total Contributions: $120,500.00

Future Value (9.00%)　　Total Contributions

Investor.gov

40 Years

Most of you have families and little ones depending on you. This is how you prepare them for their future. If the interest you're earning is less than two percent, then money is being lost, whether it's sitting in the bank or under your mattress. The charts used above isn't typical of the stock market. I am being extremely modest if we look at the charts below growing at a rate of 1.3% and as high as 37.6% (volatility). You can think of the money that has been washed down the drain as in your generational wealth. Looking at past yearly returns gives you an overview of what investing could do for your future.

Potential earnings through investing 40 Years

1.3% "1994" The year my sister was mad I crashed her prom

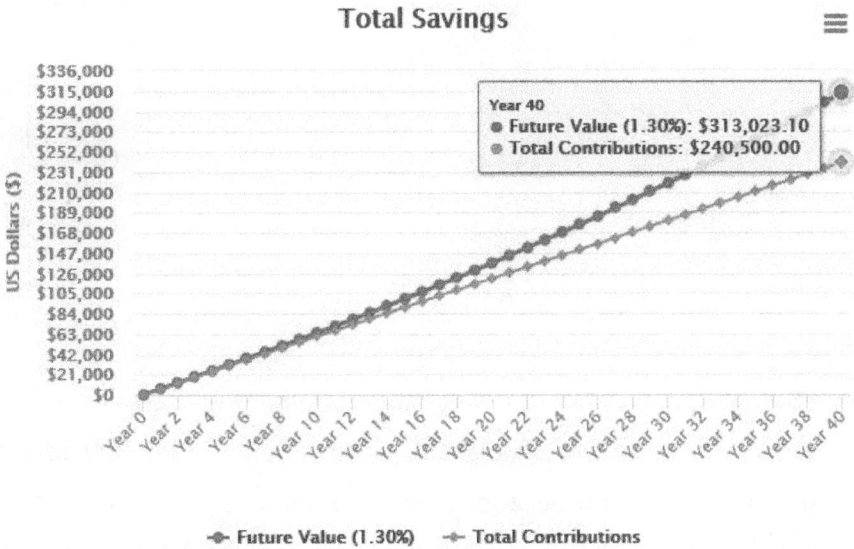

Total Savings

Year 40
● Future Value (1.30%): $313,023.10
● Total Contributions: $240,500.00

US Dollars ($)

$336,000
$315,000
$294,000
$273,000
$252,000
$231,000
$210,000
$189,000
$168,000
$147,000
$126,000
$105,000
$84,000
$63,000
$42,000
$21,000
$0

Year 0, Year 2, Year 4, Year 6, Year 8, Year 10, Year 12, Year 14, Year 16, Year 18, Year 20, Year 22, Year 24, Year 26, Year 28, Year 30, Year 32, Year 34, Year 36, Year 38, Year 40

–●– Future Value (1.30%) –+– Total Contributions

Investor.gov

You still made money through compound interest. Yes, just like with anything else, there are pros and cons. However, the pros have always outweigh the cons when it comes to the stock market. The downside is that you could hit a few rough years like 2006. But the year this angel "Me" walked across the stage, most individuals who don't look like me became filthy rich.

37.6% "1995" The year my sister didn't crash my prom

Total Savings

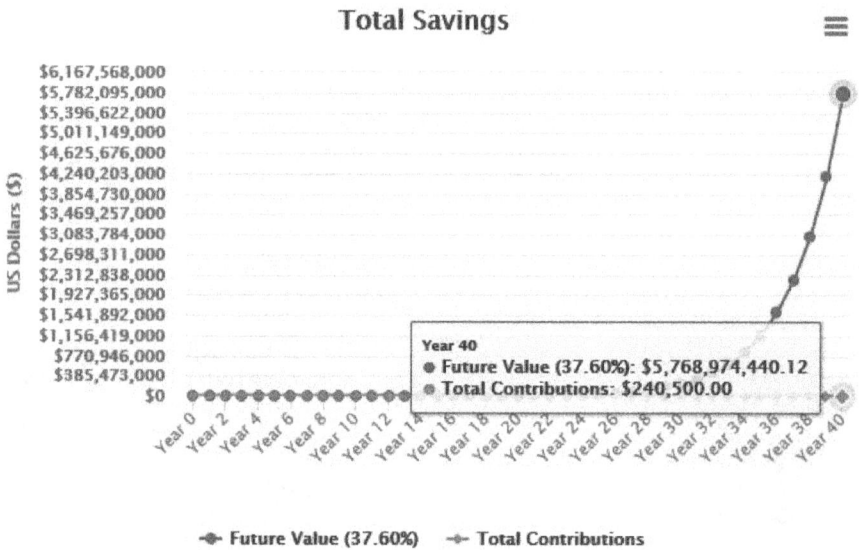

Year 40	
● Future Value (37.60%): $5,768,974,440.12	
● Total Contributions: $240,500.00	

◆ Future Value (37.60%)   ◆ Total Contributions

Investor.gov

During the .com era, if you had been investing for 40 years at a conservative rate of $500.00 a month totaling $240,000 investment dollars, you would be a millionaire six times over. I guarantee that if you had this mindset, you would have invested more throughout the years once you witnessed how your money was working for you.

Yes, I know it's depressing to see what you could have had by investing your money. I get it and I don't like seeing it either but, this is often our reality. We don't want to see the mistakes of our past and what turning up will cost us.

https://www.investor.gov/additional-resources/free-financial-planning-tools/compound-interest-calculator

Inflation – Increase of prices and fall in the purchasing value of money. The inflation rate responds to each phase of a business cycle.

Expansion – The first phase and is considered positive and healthy at a rate of 2% to 2.9%.

Peak Phase – Next up is the Peak Phase. This is when the economy expands to 3% or greater (creating what's called an asset bubble). Assets become inflated as in real estate. Remember this?

2006 – The Beginning of the Crash

Early signs of trouble first arose when some subprime loans went into default. In 2007 the market froze, and things started declining swiftly. Subprime credit stopped, interest rates increased, and consumer loans rose drastically. I'm sure that happened because middle classes needed to be bailed out but remember, there's no fund for that. Hard working American citizens had to sit back and figure it out and at the end of that decision came a personal loan with a high-ass interest rate.

Here I have pulled up a timeline of events to show you that our past will repeat itself especially since we've been here before and are here now. We must start thinking bigger or we will be at the mercy of Industry dictatorship. Corporations coming into our industry and shutting us out. Start paying attention to the economy and how it shifts. Pay attention to how it affects you. Education is at a decline in most of our family communities including the beauty industry. We must build up to build out.

Timeline of Events for 2007

February: Freddie Mac announced that they were no longer buying the riskiest subprime.

April: Subprime lender New Century Financial Corporation files for bankruptcy.

June: Bear Stearns announced a loan of 3.2 billion dollars to help bail out one of its funds that invested in collateralized debt obligations (CDOs).

July: The stock market hit a new all-high over 14,000. On July 31, Bear Stearns liquidates two of its mortgage-back security hedge funds.
August: A worldwide credit crunch had begun and there were no subprime loans available. Subprime lender American Home Mortgage files for bankruptcy. This marked the start of the **housing market crash.**

September: The Libor rate rises to its highest level since December of 1998, at 6.8%.

December: The stock market finishes the year at 13,264.

Timeline of Events for 2008

January 11: Bank of America acquired Countrywide financial for 4.1 billion dollars. Countrywide had a total of 1.5 trillion in loans.

March 16: Bear Stearns was facing bankruptcy signs a merger agreement with J.P. Morgan for $2 a share which was a fraction of the current trading price.

May 19: The markets had its final day at 13028.

September 6: The Treasury announced a takeover of both Fannie Mae and Freddie Mac that had over 5 trillion dollars in mortgages.

September 14: Bank of America signs a deal to acquire Merrill Lynch.

September 15: Lehman Brothers filed bankruptcy. The Dow drops 400 points closing at 10,917

September 17: The Federal Reserve loans $85 billion dollars to American International Group (AIG).

September 18: Fed Chairman Ben Bernanke and Treasury Secretary met with Congress proposed a $700 billion-dollar bailout. Bernanke tells Congress "If we don't do this, we may not have an economy on Monday."

September 26: Federal regulators seized Washington Mutual and then strike a deal to sell the majority of J.P. Morgan for 1.9 billion dollars. This represents the largest bank failure in U.S. history.

September 29: Congress votes against $700 billion bailout plan. That same day Citigroup attains Wachovia.

October 1: The Senate passes $700 billion bailout bill.

October 3: The house passes $700 billion bailout plan and the Obama signs it into law.

October 6: Fed announces it will provide $900 billion in short-term loans to banks. The Dow closes below 10,000.

October 7: The fed announced it will lend roughly 1.3 trillion dollars to companies outside the banking sector.

October 10: The stock market had its worst week ever losing 22% over 8 trading days or 8.4 trillion dollars from the market highs in 2007.

October 14: The Treasury taps $250 billion of bailout funds and used the money to maintain the top banks.

December 31: Over 3 million foreclosures by the end of the year. Michigan, Florida, Arizona and California had rates of 4% with Nevada at 7.3%. 75 % spike from the previous year.

The Aftermath

Even though the financial crisis was resolved by the start of 2009 the housing market continued to decline. There were over three million foreclosure filings for 2009. Unemployment rose over 10% and the housing market crash created the worst recession since the 1980's. By the 4th quarter of 2009, the inexperienced significant GDP growth and corporate earnings had increased by over 100%. The Unemployment Rate had stabilized towards the end of 2009.
www.stockpickssystem.com/housing-market-crash-2007

Wealthy people mess up all the time and they take us down with them. What they do differently is because of what they've learned differently.

Chapter 7

The Wake-Up Call

In twenty years, how old will you be? In forty years, how old will your children be? Financial freedom is earned through time and having a little patience will set you up for life. Being cute and fly should be done at an affordable rate and not at the cost of your lifetime income.

Making a million dollars simply starts with a mindset. Change your mindset and change your bank account.

Two things you should understand about the Stock Market:

1. It will always be bailed out (at least it has been in the past)
2. It is volatile but worth it

Hiring a financial adviser is a must however research is necessary for all millionaire strategies.

<u>Mall Kiosk</u>

This Strategy can be done with salon personnel or collaborating with a freelance artist.

Find creative ways to set up shop inside a busy mall. Kiosk aren't cheap and they need to be mapped out perfectly with your marketing and business development strategist. Kiosks can range from $3,500.00 - $6,000.00 dollars a month and can be a gold mine if you offer the right services and or sell the right products.

As a hairstylist you could make upwards of $1,500.00 - $2,500.00 dollars a day. Negotiating skills and being laser focused on your target audience is required. Only your best stylists and employees should be there to represent. No slackers or you will make no money. Malls typically open at 10:00am during the week and up until 9:00pm – 10:00pm. Customer service should come naturally to you and your team. Being energetic and having an awesome kiosk will attract potential customers. Having a key marketing strategy and learning the analytics of your traffic flow to your kiosk can be rinsed and repeated throughout different mall locations. Investing into your core business means leveraging everything you have. If you have the coins, invest it in a great team and watch your money grow. If you're running a successful high-traffic kiosk, you can earn between $45,000.00 - $75,000.99 a month which is $540,000.00 - $900,000.00 dollars. That's $100,000.00 dollars shy of one million.

All strategies in this book aren't meant to create financial freedom for you. It's meant to create financial freedom to a starving community of talented artists. Some of these strategies will inspire you to connect and pool your funds together under the proper business structure. We aren't talking taking risk with scam artists. You should verify first and trust later. Business is always business and you want to always operate from black and white. Everything is put in writing. #period

What is your Think Different?

- Play your position, not your opposition

and stop trying to be like everyone else. Particularly, since people pay for different.

How will you ever win a fight by imitating your opponent? That is how you should treat your business. Different in your own perspective and no one else's. People attach themselves to brands.

So, what is it about you that should be remembered?

The name of your company is a perfect example. Don't get too complicated in your name because there will be plenty of time to be fancy but not now. Clean, simple, meaningful and/or powerful is what you want to strive for.

For Example:

1. Budget Rental Car
2. Giant foods
3. PayPal

These business name examples leave no room for confusion. They are direct and the names can be concluded as winners.

Mock Game - Lets Play

Please draw a line to the answer that best describes each business.

Giant Foods	Renting a car on a budget
PayPal	Chronically hair in a studio
Budget Rental Car	The Giant of Foods
Hair Chronicles Studio	Pay your Pals

How did you do?

Spelling is also a factor when choosing a name. No one is going to spend hours, minutes or seconds googling a made-up name that's pronounced Tricks but spelled like: Trix, Trixx, Triks, or Trixxx. In some cases, people have built a social media following with their name alone and become local celebrities. If that's you, that is freaking Awesome! I applaud you and clearly want you to know that you are doing something right. However, there might come a day when you will have to choose between keeping what you've built or rebranding to attract a global and/or international market.

Of course, you can cross that bridge when you get there. Nevertheless, if this isn't your authentic style, rebranding can be costly unless you have the capital to educate your target audience. My suggestion would be to rebrand sooner than later if you plan to scale. You want to make it user friendly and hassle free for your customers to find you. With so many platforms to follow don't overthink your name. Getting too creative here can put a wedge between you and your bottom line and you won't even know it. All because they just simply forgot your name or how to spell it. When something as simple as the name of your company becomes an education lesson for your prospective client, you move further and further away from the finish line. The spelling in your name needs no big personality. No need for change if it's working for you. The important thing here is to be creative and stay focused on the bigger picture. That is your mission.

Are you trying to stay Local or transition to Mogul?

Your name is what the world hears. Your logo is what the world sees.

Allow me to re-introduce myself (in my Jay-Z voice). You can either enter the conversation or become the conversation. I'll take become the   conversation   for $20,000.00   Alex

JEOPARDY!

If the people around you and strangers are always complimenting your logo then you've become the conversation. What that normally means is that when introduced to the world, they will make you a part of the conversation. Conversation is all talk no bang and here is where you put your heart and soul!

Your Mission

This is a big deal so don't spend all your time picking out names, wall colors and floors. The main focus should be your mission.

1. What value are you bringing to the world?
2. What do you stand for?

If it isn't good enough or strong enough, modify and convey it in a different way. This is your heart on paper. Have a mission that resonates to your ideal customer. In some cases, you might need to hire a copywriter to write a sales script that hits home.

Powerful Mission Statements

American Express: We work hard every day to make American Express the world's most respected service brand.

Bold, straight to the point and nothing fancy. American Express is for a very exclusive crowd.

Nordstrom: To give customers the most compelling shopping experience possible.

I think they've lived up to their mission statement. Anything you buy, you can return forever.

Ted Talks: Spread Ideas

People are fascinated with ideas. We love to be inspired.

www.blog.hubspot.com

Hair Chronicles Studio: Creating leverage for behind-the-chair stylist.

Starting the conversation brings enlightenment.

The key to wealth isn't about money it must be about something bigger.

Who do You want to Save?

Maybe it's your family, business, dog, the world or yourself. For me it's the beauty industry for the everyday hairstylist who built it. Maybe you would like to live in a world where everyone has clean water. No matter what your dream is, be on fire and chase it. This is where you find out what you're made of and you need sustainability to do so.

Will it take money?

Money is essential in our daily lives. It will take devising a plan and getting rid of wasteful habits that can set you up for a lifetime. The more people you connect with, the more opportunities you gain for potential customers.

Time Management

There are only 24-hours in a day which limits how many heads you can slay before you pass out. Don't be afraid to ask for help!

The power of one will kill your business. Starting alone is fine but staying alone will drain your resources. Focus more on your strong areas of business and delegate the rest to someone who specializes in that field.

Knowing the LV (Lifetime Value) of your customer

This number isn't etched in stone but a very important aspect of building a valuable customer roster. When a customer graduates to a client that means he/she is loyal to your brand. They come faithfully once a week, twice a month or every two months. The point is that they have a consistent schedule. Your customer has valued you and the services that's being provided to them. Don't mess this up by taking advantage of your customer and abusing their time. This happens too often in our industry and in today's world, our time is precious and cannot afford to be wasted. Start to become more inclusive, offering the services your clients want. Being able to pamper your client with an abundance of positive energy and love is priceless and a rarity that many would pay for.

<u>**Understanding the LV**</u>

If you have a client that sits in your chair four times a month at $60.00 for each service, that totals $240.00 a month x 12 = $2,888.00 a year from one client. Now, being realistic, this scenario is rare. In fact, I have never had a client that came to me more than twice and continued to repeat that same service over and over. As a stylist, I'm sure you can relate. So, now let's add in relaxers, color, treatments, trims, cuts, highlights, keratin, extensions etc. These extra fees can average between $450.00 – $600.00 a month x 12 = $5,400.00 to $7,200.00 annually.

This is considered a behind the chair strategy because this is where you will spend your time. Now you can do the math the same to get your own figures.

One client equals approximately $7,200.00 dollars a year. Most hairstylists see an average of three clients a day for 24 days out of the month and that averages 72 clients a month. The totals can range between $388,000.00 – $518,000.00 depending on how much is charged. Some stylist charge more and see more clients a day. If you are taking this route and not wasting your money on too many things that will not pour back into your business, you can become a shear millionaire in 2 - 3½ years.

This is just the tip of the iceberg

Imagine this:

- You go into operation "money is not my biggest motivator" and start minding your business.
- You set up a strategic plan on gaining more exposure and connecting with your target audience.
- You've added additional services which brings in a different clientele.

- Your monthly clientele grows to 95 clients with average tickets of $650.00 for adding extensions.
- You now average four clients a day.
- Your yearly revenue totals over $741,000.00.

This one equation can be tailored to your own calculations. By becoming a specialty stylist, you can position yourself differently and charge what you're worth. Some hairstylist charge $2000.00 for a custom-made weave installation. If you book two services a day, you would net over 1.4 million dollars in a year.

Although it is important to know your numbers, it is essential to understand the potential value of growing a clientele over a customer base. Start by treating your clients like family and eventually they will become one.

Price + Commitment + Purpose = High Quality Clients!

If you want high quality clients, become a stylist in demand offering the best products. Showcase your amazing skills and you will be respected as a professional, not just a person who does hair.

If money is your biggest motivator, you will lose focus of customer request. Slow down and create an experience. Go back to the time when you said how your salon will be different and honor that.

Creative Event Packages

Collaborate with other freelance professionals and organize monthly, quarterly or yearly events. This is not just a party or a simple networking event. These events should be well-orchestrated, properly planned, marketed and executed. Organizing events for your clients, community or to raise funds can be extremely fun and lucrative. We all have had our share of unprofessional hair shows and beauty expose'. This will not be you. Yours will count and they may even cost a pretty penny, but it will be so worth it. Is this your area of expertise? Having an event where hundreds of people will attend can be extremely profitable. Hosting can yield some high returns on your investment. Business Leaders collaborate for a reason and so can you.

Freelance professionals are always looking for an opportunity to showcase their work. Provide them a platform to do so.

Hosting an event like a hair show can introduce you to major opportunities. Of course, your event does not have to be limited to a hair show. You can organize all types of events that are suitable for your target audience on so many levels so let your creative juices flow.

Let me first say that everything you do should be strategically planned when it comes to putting money on the table. Make sure to have the best team on board and do your research. Imagine an upscale masquerade theme hair show given at a popular art gallery in the ritziest part of town. Once you decide on the venue, your vision comes to life. Your mind's made up and now it's time to put it into action. There should be no turning back.

- Will it be a day or night event?
- Will I need to hire a deejay?
- What will my menu look like (i.e., crab cakes or lamb chops)?

Carefully comb through every detail to see if it's worth it. Taking every concept into consideration and playing out different scenarios is how you beat your opposition. Understanding how motivated and determined you are, wholeheartedly set the date. Ok, so October 31st will be perfect, and I will take it (venue) for whopping $3,500.00.

YOU GOT THIS!

You got this, and God has You!

Let's map out your expenses and go over the bomb-ass pricing structure based on your financials:

- Venue - $3,500.00
- Food - $4,000.00
- Décor - $1,500.00
- Promotional and miscellaneous items - $2,500.00
- Stage $1,000.00

Total for this Masquerade Hair Show = $12,500.00

Initial deposits to lock everything in place = $5,000.00

You would like a long red runway gracing the stage with seating on each side. Your tickets range from $75.00 (general admission) to $250.00 (front row seats).

- Vendor tables are $200.00 x 10 = $2,000.00
- Tickets at $75.00 x 140 = $10,500.00
- Tickets at $125.00 x 40 = $5,000.00
- Tickets at $175.00 x 80 = $14,000.00
- Tickets at $250 x 40 = $10,000.00
- Total Ticket Revenue if all tickets sold = $41,000.00

Minus the $5000.00 you paid for your deposit and paying the balance of $7,500.00.

ROI (return on investment) = $28,000.00

I know you might be saying: *it's easier said than done,* however becoming a millionaire isn't easy either but somehow there are an estimated 400,000 new millionaires every year. What is stopping you from being one?

Here is where most stylist go wrong, believing time is on their side and it isn't. Time can't be replenished. Time is so precious because you can't get it back and once it runs out game over. You are now on the clock and promoting day in and day out is necessary and having a strong marketing and social media team is a must. Unlike growing a clientele through referrals throwing an upscale event will be different. This particular fee structure can be done with other equations. There are hundreds of events happening right now that people have paid tens of thousands of dollars to attend. Strategy isn't a matter of when it's a matter of how.

Growing your business from behind the chair starts with ditching a loser's mindset.

No more setting limits on yourself and making excuses.

No more playing defense with your money believing that holding on to it will make it last longer when actually, you're losing money every day.

Be humble for the things you have achieved and to pass that on you must unleash your rich mindset.

Playing offense with your dollars, understanding you must make more money. What you believe you achieve. If you wake up every day and put a limit on yourself, you've already lost. The true value in life is knowing your worth after embracing that, making a million dollars will be introduced to the "to do list".

You must dream globally but win locally.

Having a dream means more than just surviving today you need to evolve through the decades.

If you try to run a business off a short-term plan with no long term goals you will fail. People follow visionaries not companies.

Your number one goal as a leader is to see the future. We celebrate today but understanding its short lived.

Realizing right now we struggle but knowing victory is right around the corner.

If you're trying to be a boss and build a team the odds are you won't be effective. Bosses don't lead they delegate, dictate and spectate. Leaders create the example you want your team to lead by.

Being able to build financial wealth can be lonely, difficult and it will test your mental state like no other. For every positive thought there are thousands of negative thoughts. Your mind will literally shut you down. You must pull that positive energy from your heart, soul and the divine spirit. No one has the permission to tell you you're not good enough.

Change your mindset change your bank account.

Memberships

Memberships can be designed to fit into any payment structure already in place. Establishing a membership program can open a recurring stream of revenue and doing less work behind the chair. As a hairstylist I'm sure you can think of so many ways to customize packages. Samples of the newest products, free services, merchandise giveaways, birthday club, VIP club how many do you think will sign up for an after hours membership. Be creative you stand to make a million dollars with this strategy.

What can you offer 5000 people (clients or not) that can pay you 17.00 a month for one year?

When you find out you can earn 1,020,000 million dollars.

2000 people @ 42.00 = $1,008,000.00

1000 people @ 83.00 = $996,000.00

500 people @ 167.00 = $1,002,000.00

300 people @ 278.00 = $1,000,800.00

Monthly fees can add up just like Birchbox, Hulu and Netflix. Over 200 million users and these companies are netting over a billion dollars. Find something that can truly engage your customers and keep them happy. Offering a membership service can be tailored any way you see fit. You might want to offer a $5.99 bang trimming services for kids ages 4 to 13 and make your million in 18 months. The point is becoming a millionaire is all how you play with numbers. By the way, I think this is an awesome idea. I always strategize from a different angle.

Online Store

Selling retail online is an absolute must and because the market is so broad you can create a different online profile carrying an array of products.

Shopping online isn't going anywhere anytime soon. Find your voice and open an online store. Selling trendy items can be a hit. I know you remember the fidget spinner craze. They bought in over 500,000,000 million dollars. Those who had fidget spinners as part of their inventory doubled down and watch the cash roll in. In today's market opening an online store can be done through amazon, eBay, Etsy, Shopify and so many others including Facebook and Instagram.

Having a professional e-commerce store separates you from other artists that are simply working behind the chair. Retail is the bulk of any business not service. Make sure to offer items that are cohesive with your brand and well packaged. Finding ways to earn multiple streams of income will help you build stability with your finances. Carrying a $2000.00 bag with no savings or life insurance for you and your family are sure signs of being in a WannaBe and TrynaBe phase. Your mindset must think about the future and stop living just for today.

Most of us are completely attached to our phones and the way of the world tells us that e-commerce is just getting started and it isn't too late to join the team.

When starting an online business, understand that there are only two types of businesses:

1. Service Based
2. Product Based

Service based is a business we all should be familiar with. It's what we do to make the most of our income. Styling hair, painting nails, applying make-up and so many others. We can make money instantly by exchanging services. It's also easy to capitalize on other areas of the industry when you're not servicing a client. Becoming an online consultant or offering classes are service based as well.

Teaching advanced courses to up-and-coming stylists can be fulfilling and exceedingly rewarding. I highly recommend that you focus on being knowledgeable in what you want to become your area of expertise. No one wants to spend hard earned money with an opportunist. Something else people aren't spending money on are brick and mortar locations.

I almost went that route myself. I thought I needed to open a physical location but once I realized my target audience was online, I had to switch my game plan. The startup cost for having an online business is astronomically different from the upfront cost to have a physical location. I suggest making sure you know exactly where your target audience is before making such a concrete decision.

Chapter 8

Breaking Forth

Starting any business is equivalent to having a baby. So plan to explore:

1. **Organizational Ones**
2. **Trial and Error Twos**
3. **Think Tank threes**
4. **Finance and Formalities Fours**
5. **Freedom through Failure Fives**

<u>**Organizational Ones**</u>

Building an organization of any kind can be a daunting task. Having structure, patience and staying motivated is necessary to prevail. Here is where personalities can clash so take heart to the saying: *Too many Chiefs and not enough Indians.* You should be the only chief unless you're in a partnership which at that time, devise a strategy to figure it out. It is always great to hear different perspectives, however, choose the road you will least regret. Again, even if it's the wrong road, it's still the right road because you were able to learn what not to do.

Trial and Error Twos

We can discuss several topics here, but I think revenue can show up on the list more than once. Expect to waste plenty of money if you do not have a road map. Budgeting is necessary and helps to minimize cash flow problems. Never make the purchase unless you know for sure it's the best deal. Scammers are always in business and love fresh meat to take advantage of. Research ways to conserve money on salon projects, miscellaneous items and payroll cost. Work with suppliers to receive discounts on bulk orders. In the early stages of your business development, recognize what part of your business you can outsource.

Think Tank Threes

Facilitating Think Tank workshops are a way to expound on your vision and watching it come to fruition with a stellar team. This is what some call a round table meeting of the minds. Solid ideas can be bred here. I researched and found the strategy of Frost & Sullivan. This strategy can be used when conducting your Think Tank Dream Team sessions.

Effective Think Tank Session Facilitation Techniques

1. Introduce Think Tank Session (Time: 10 minutes)
   a. Define the Think Tank Session for the participants:

There is a formal agenda set by the facilitator. Specific group activities and exercises are incorporated to stimulate the exchange of ideas and to allow for participants to problem-solve approaches to common problems.

b. Define your role as facilitator:

This is where you set the agenda and expectations for session outcomes (what we will cover and the take-a-ways) like:

- Managing group discussion dynamics
- Engagement from all group members in the discussion
- Working with smaller groups to challenge thinking, share ideas, restate ideas
- Create lists and
- Summarize and conclude discussion

c. Explain to participants' their role and responsibility to participate effectively:

DO:

- Ask a question when you have one
- Feel free to share an illustration
- Request an example if a point is not clear
- Search for ways in which you can apply a general principle or idea to your work
- Think of ways you can pass on ideas to your subordinates
- Be skeptical ... don't buy everything you hear

DON'T:

- Close your mind by saying, "This is all fine in theory, but..."
- Assume that all topics covered will be equally relevant to your needs

2. Conduct Think Tank Session
    a. Poll the audience ... ask for a show of hands to determine audience profile (e.g., vendor, practitioner, functional role in company, etc.)

    b. Break the audience into smaller groups to foster networking and problem solving, perhaps based on a common profile or interest.

    c. Introduce the first issue or pose the first question for the smaller groups to brainstorm.

- The issue or question should be structured, e.g., (list two drawbacks, list two upsides, list two challenges to "X"; explain how "X" applies to your company, etc.)
- Assign a specific time period for the group to brainstorm
- Advise groups they will be debriefed, and tell them to write down ideas and identify a spokesperson
- Move around from group to group to listen in on discussions or provoke discussion and answer questions
- With three minutes left, advise the groups to wrap up

    d. Debrief the groups. Ask what each group came up with, going from point to point, one group to another – this facilitates interaction between the groups

    e. Track the group learning's by utilizing a flipchart to illustrate what is emerging from the brainstorming

    f. Contribute value-added commentary

    g. Introduce the next issue, and proceed as above

3. Conclude Think Tank Session

    a. Summarize the agenda items and the key issues that emerged

    b. Ask the group if they wish to share key insights of what they've gained

    c. Ask if any individuals wish to share key items they will action upon when they return to office

    d. Advise your team you will prepare a written summary of the session to be posted on the event. Encourage the group to continue an electronic discussion post-even

    e. Add any concluding remarks.

Think Tanks are normally comprised of intellectuals however this can be customized based on our industry. Outside of your bookworms, consider having a creative bunch, an analytical crew and some know-it-all's. The more artistic your team, the better your chances are in producing valuable data.

FYI: Some Think Tanks are publicly traded companies on the stock market, and this too can be a multimillion-dollar industry. This can be an innovative task for a group to take on but when you do (count me in). A Think Tank of creative, trendsetting beauty professionals sounds awesome to me. I have listed a few successful Think Tank industries below the Golden Key you should research especially if this is something that attracts your interest.

Build a one-of-a-kind Think Tank group. People in business pay serious cash to a group of individuals to think up some stuff.

Kaiser Family Foundation

Founded in 1948, the Kaiser Family Foundation focuses on major healthcare issues in the US and, to a lesser extent, the world. Over the years, it has become a must-read for healthcare devotees and a quality non-partisan source for up-to-date and accurate information on health policy. The Foundation regularly releases facts, polls, and analyses that are in turn used by the media, policymakers, the healthcare community, and the general public. Specific research programs include disparities policy, global health policy, health costs, health reform, HIV/AIDS, Medicaid, Medicare, private insurance, the uninsured, and women's health policy. Despite an original association, the Foundation is no longer affiliated with Kaiser Permanente or Kaiser Industries.

- Political Orientation: Independent
- SEMrush Ranking: 7.0K
- Monthly Traffic: 182K
- Monetary Value of Monthly Traffic: $356,000
- Average Yearly Revenue: $127 million
- Average Media References per Year (by Others): 874
- 2014 Global Go To Think Tank Index Report Rankings: None
- Notable Figures: Drew Altman, Diane Rowland, Mollyann Brodie

Epic

The Electronic Privacy Information Center, also known as EPIC, was founded in 1994 by the Fund for Constitutional Government and Computer Professionals for Social Responsibility. At first, EPIC focused solely on government surveillance and issues having to do with cryptology. Since then, it has expanded to include programs and research on a much wider variety of topics, including government transparency, electronic voting, identity theft, medical record privacy, commercial mining data, and the use of the Freedom of Information Act to publicize documents. Appropriately, EPIC's publications are practically all online. In addition to maintaining websites and groups such as privacy.org, the Public Voice coalition, and the Privacy Coalition, EPIC publishes the online EPIC Alert every two weeks. Other EPIC publications include *Privacy & Human Rights, Litigation Under the Federal Open Government Laws, Public Voice WSIS Sourcebook, Privacy Law Sourcebook,* and *Consumer Law Sourcebook.*

- Political Orientation: Libertarian
- SEMrush Ranking: 27.6K
- Monthly Traffic: 38.1K
- Monetary Value of Monthly Traffic: $99,200
- Average Yearly Revenue: $805,000
- Average Media References per Year (by Others): 275
- 2014 Global Go To Think Tank Index Report Rankings: None

https://thebestschools.org/features/most-influential-think-tanks/

Having a great mind and understanding systems, concepts and people can be a sure way of life while creating financial freedom. By now your mind should be tossing around its own million-dollar ideas.

Finance and Formalities Fours

As a startup you can't overlook the importance of how your cash flow is managed. Most shy away from this subject and that is something you can't do. Knowing your numbers are key. Everything rises and falls with you so there is no "I didn't know". You must know everything going on in your business especially with your money. How else will you know when you've reached a million dollars? This *early in the game revenue generation* might not be accessible, nonetheless you need to know if your business is losing money. As a creative we tend to trust then verify instead of the other way around. Make sure everyone on your team is someone you can trust, especially anyone that handles or deals with any cash/credit transactions. No matter how deep that trust goes, this is your baby and you must treat it as such. We've all heard the rumors of Lindsey Lohan's parents. Your bookkeeper can be your sister, accountant and even your brother but it doesn't matter. This is your baby and you as the guardian should know its complete history. Your business is new to this world. It's fragile and can't stand on its own. You must guide it every step of the way. To leave it in someone else's hands can be considered as neglect or abandonment. This is the newborn phase and you don't need a babysitter. There are no nights off and no more sleeping in until noon. Introducing a new business to the world and not knowing its numbers is equivalent to carrying a baby for 40 weeks, having contractions and then going through natural childbirth on the same day.

One of the reasons salons barely market or don't market at all has a lot to do with not understanding financial management which leads to not knowing your **customer acquisition cost** (every dollar you spend to acquire your client). Knowing how much it takes to get a client in your chair will shed light on what your **(ROI)** return on investment (profit gained) should be.

Most online businesses can range from 0-50 dollars so there's really no excuse. Remember this isn't a race to the finish line. It's a mindset that I crossed the finish line. Go at a pace that is most effective for you while setting realistic deadlines. Ten years ago, I was popping bottles in Miami chilling on the beach with wifey for two weeks. We literally had no care in the world. Our lives were set until life showed up. I stress the severity of creating multiple streams of income, learn and teach your kids about money even though financial literacy is lacking in beauty school curriculum. We all know that to make money you must spend money.

Well, this is a crash course on what is needed to become wealthy and having that awareness will set you up for success.

This is different than startup cost. Why? Because startup cost is needed to create the business in the first place. Without spending these funds your business will be non-existent. Make sure items purchased are what you need in Phase 1. From there go into Phase 2 and Phase 3 and so forth and so on.

Freedom through Failure Fives

I'm not going to sit here and tell you this stuff isn't painstakingly difficult, or it doesn't hurt like hell. I mean like end of the world tears and that's why the dream test is necessary. You are drawn to it (fear) and like Rocky and Adrian (No Matter What) you must go through it and knock the heck out it. Failure is only an obstacle. It frees you from a path of consecutive mistakes what some might deem the domino effect. It's learning your receptionist has been skimming off the top and firing her ASAP! Sure, you could be passive aggressive and give her another chance, blame someone else for not doing a proper screening and stand there soaking because you failed to see this setback coming. **Why do you allow yourself to stay here?** Hold no grudges this is where you're supposed to be. Like Moses, it's time to lead your people to the promise land. Holding grudges will waste time and money, and neither can you afford to lose.

Real Estate

We've all heard the phrase flipping houses and know at least one person with one or more investment properties. Real Estate is another investment that requires upfront cost most of the time. Some have mastered the art of purchasing properties through debt (which I think is genius). Basically, instead of buying shoes and bags use your credit card to buy a house.

Robert Kiyosaki- Bestselling Author of Rich Dad Poor Dad

He has written many books that will span the test of time however this book surpasses them all. A little background of the book, Rich Dad is based on the father of his best friend and Poor Dad is based on his father. He clearly admired his Rich Dad's life and was determined to learn the strategy he used to do it. One of his breakthrough moments came from a conversation.

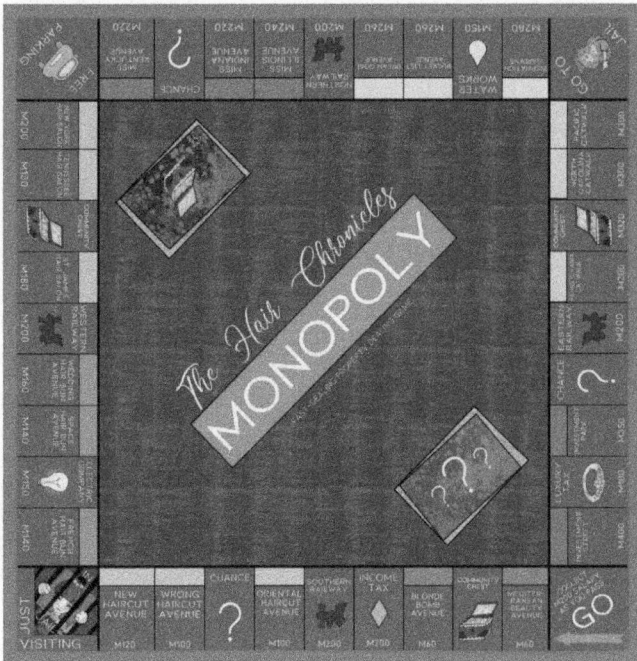

His Rich Dad explained; you must invest in Real Estate.

The Dialogue

Robert: *Real Estate, Why?*

Rich Dad: *Well, four green houses and one red hotel*

Robert: *Yeah but, aren't you going to teach me?*

Rich Dad: *I don't have time to teach idiots. That's not my job. Your job is to be a student, then I'll teach you.* (Rich Dad really believes in Education)

Robert: While in the Marine Corp watching television in Hawaii, an advertisement came across the TV. *Learn how to invest in Real Estate with no money down* so he signed up.

The man in the commercial goes on to say "You see the beauty about Real Estate is that you learn to use debt to get rich. If you're going to be rich you must learn how to use debt. It's called using other people's money. So, when I hear poor people say to me "I don't have any money" I say, "It's because you're not supposed to use your money! You're supposed to use other people's money.""

(Day one) Instructor says to thirty of us in the class "this is your assignment, and this is where you get your education. You are required to look at 100 properties in ninety days and do a write-up of those properties." Thirty days in, half the class had quit. By sixty days the other half had quit. In the final days it was six of us left and all of us went on to become multi-millionaires. People are poor because they quit or give up too soon.

When he finally reviews all the properties, he realizes what property he wanted to buy. It was a foreclosed beachfront condo in Maui.

Robert: *How much is a one-bedroom condominium?*

Gentleman: $18,000.00

Robert: *How much is the down payment?*

Gentleman: 10%

Robert: *Can I put it on a credit card?*

Gentleman: *Yes, you can*

He finishes by stating his first property was 100% debt and that this course was the best education he ever had.

This strategy is one of many when it comes to Real Estate. Finding a mentor or doing proper research on your market and demographics can line your pockets like no other.

You must be willing to the commitment of completing all strategies in this book. Don't be like the people who quit before they could understand the lesson. Everything isn't for everybody. However, I am sure some of you will be awesome at this. I hear often that it can be fun, and I know sometimes looking at houses online can be a unique experience.

Flipping vs Renting

Flipping houses would be considered passive income taking very little of your effort.

Renting property is active income. It will eventually require some day-to-day operation.

Flipping houses is a full-fledged business. It is also **speculation** of engaging in risky transactions in hopes of gaining a profit from market evaluations. You can earn thousands to hundreds of thousands in one sale, depending on the goals you set with a financial advisor or your accountant.

Research shows your tax expenses can range from 25%-43% per sale.

Make sure you meet the requirements for your state.

Deciding to flip houses is not a long-term commitment. After all requirements are met you simply put it on the market and wait for it to sell.

Making the decision to have rental properties can be a lot of time and work. When you are in between tenants the mortgage still needs to be paid, upkeep must be done, and inspections and regulations must be met. It also ties into why multiple streams of income is important to have. In any business rainy days will visit and often overstay their welcome. In this section you absolutely need a stash of cash remember this too can be an investment group.

Project Management might be needed as well to oversee rental responsibilities, maintenance, repairs, budget and records, just to name a few.

Owning rental properties is considered passive income because once you have a responsible tenant you can sit back and collect a monthly check.

Landlords can choose to have a lease from 1-5 years. If a tenant pays $2,500.00.00 a month on a three-year lease you stand to gain $90,000.00 over the lease period.

After paying your mortgage of $1,300.00, your monthly profit is $1,200.00. An additional $14,400.00.00 dollars a year and $43,200.00 over the lease period.

One house can net you more than the average person's income.

Most millionaires that are successful in Real Estate have multiple properties all over the world and since we are talking millionaire strategies let's look at your future projections.

Your investment club proudly owns twenty properties in the United States and two Internationally. The numbers below reflect monthly profit after expenses. Here is a list of your properties and profits;

US Properties	International Properties
(3) Washington DC - $7,000.00	Ontario, Canada - $3,000.00
(2) Miami, Florida - $1,2700.00	Toronto, Canada - $1,400.00
Orlando, Florida - $1,200.00	
Greensville, North Carolina - $1,700.00	
76,922 x 12= 923,064 Total	
Charlotte, North Carolina - $2,722.00	
Greensboro, North Carolina - $2,100.00	
Bowie, Maryland - $2,000.00	
Waldorf, Maryland - $1,800.00	
(2) Baltimore, Maryland - $4,500.00	
Outerbanks, South Carolina - $10,000.00	

(3) Atlanta, Georgia - $8,500.00	
New Orleans, Louisiana - $3,000.00	
(2) Detroit Michigan - $2,700.00	

Again, this isn't about crossing the finish line first. It's a numbers game. Buy one property while you're investing, and you can always use debt to purchase your property. Do your research and make sure you are in trustworthy ventures.

CHAPTER 9

UNCONVENTIONAL EARNINGS

<u>Cannabis</u>

In case you've been under a rock for the past few years, Cannabis is big business and, in the years to come, it will become even bigger.

- Recreational marijuana is legal is 9 states plus Washington DC.

- Medical marijuana is legal in 30 states plus Washington DC.
- 16 states welcome CBD oil and 4 states none.

MARIJUANA LEGALIZATION IN THE U.S.

STATES WITH MARIJUANA LAWS:
- FOR RECREATIONAL USE
- FOR MEDICAL USE

All are still prohibited by federal laws which makes it extremely difficult to capitalize on unless you find ways to make profits without touching the plant better known as ancillary businesses, (i.e., packaging, labeling, magazine and website offering education, entertainment, etc.).

Cannabis has grown over 30% since 2016 and it's time to catch up on this latest trend. I have seen all types of cannabis propaganda; however, does it matter that they're all making money. From penny stocks to building a financial empire in Colorado, investing in cannabis can be a sure path to financial freedom.

Medical cannabis must be prescribed by a licensed physician.

Recreational means any legal adult in any legal state can legally purchase the plant.

Some say it's a drug since a person can be arrested for possessing it, but I disagree since its biological makeup is dirt, water and a seed like most herbs and spices.

Finding ways to explore this strategy can include unique apparel, an everything you need cannabis kit, trays, money clips, robes, sleepers, and I hope you get my point. By, 2025 cannabis consumption will produce over 140 billion dollars. Stepping into this territory will take plenty of knowledge and as with all strategies, research is required.

The Power of Attraction

If you can understand its gravitational pull you would stand dead center in its path. We all know people are attracted to people and this truth is why we are building businesses. An example would be that the hairstyles we produce attracts people to our chairs.

The law of attraction works the exact same with money.

I would find myself saying, *you must spend money to make money* but learning from my experiences, I must say today, *that you will make money before ever earning one cent.*

How do you become the MVP of your business?

The first is "Mastering your Mindset". Establishing accountability for the words you use and ditching the bull you frequently believe like: "I can't do this, or I have kids, etc." The power of will can change your mindset and open doors for you.

We have talked about vision throughout this book but what we haven't covered is:

Persistence the ability to keep moving even when the head winds push you back. Don't someday yourself out of dream. Persistence is what pays off.

Cash Flow Quadrants

E   B

S   I

Employee	Big Business	Self Employed	Investor
(Has Job)	(Has System)	(Is the Job)	(Money Works)

Small Business

Each quadrant has advantages and disadvantages. In each you can stay broke or become wealthy. This goes back to why mindset is important.

Each offers its own benefits.

Employee offers security and professional benefits, which is a priority over being financial free.

Self-employed people love to work for themselves and typically answer to no one. Independence and freedom are top priority.

Big business & **I**nvestor financial Freedom and scaling businesses is their main concern.

The left side of the quadrant is continuously declining. As an employee if you have no hours to work you won't receive a paycheck. Commission and hourly stylist are in this quadrant. This isn't to say they don't make money. What is being communicated here, is that you must take the money earned and throw it over to the other side (B&I) to catch major returns. Most of us stay too long in the business of making money instead of allowing it to work for us.

While we spend our days looking cute, we are wasting valuable time on actually growing wealth.

Spend Time

Let's focus on both keywords:

Spend - Pay Out

Time - A point of time as measured in hours, minutes and minutes past.

Normally when you think of paying out, things like for a car, clothes, bags, shoes and eating comes to mind. You place the value on the money spent.

Savings isn't being valued even though it too, is being spent. As a hairstylist I always *say time is money* for different reasons, but time is time and it is the one thing that rich people buy. If you don't value your time you won't become a millionaire.

The truth about time is you must be conscious of not wasting it. With time, you must be strategic about how you spend it.

Sure, you can take classes to sharpen your skills but make sure it's not because you feel like it's needed to transcend your business. What is needed is a different mindset. Start viewing time as an asset to something you need to make money because the truth is: *we can always make more money, but we can never get back wasted time.*

Beginning now, you can make up for wasted time. Try taking on one more client or learn one more technique. This isn't going to give you the freedom or lifestyle that you desire. It's going to make you a slave to work harder for the worst kind of money. Money that doesn't give you freedom. Find out where you truly love spending your time and see how it can add value to the world, to your clients and to your business.

As hairstylists, we are taught that image is everything and the truth is: *It Does Matter!* Everyone wants to look and smell like money even if they are hiding behind a mask of truth! Entering a new chapter means embracing new tricks, playing by different rules, becoming disciplined, making sacrifices, and the ultimate: *Leveling Up.*

Millionaires read and learn a lot. Their life consists of learning what doesn't work so they can create something that will. Some of you purchased this book looking for a short-cut to wealth or some get rich scheme and there just isn't one. I looked and have done my due diligence and it just didn't pay off. With the potential income hairstylist earn per year, investing 20% of your income is something you can't afford to put off. Some of you can afford to do more and you should.

But savings isn't enough. Savings is considered neutral territory between checking and investing. It's the place where the middle child dwells. Always getting pushed to the side and then suddenly, they need you and of course, you're there for them in their time of need. Time is no longer neutral the minute it is removed. It dwindles in checking or can transcend with investing. Decreasing your expenses will give you the power to understand exactly what it means to save to invest.

x 2 – Start a Blog

We all have crazy stories and weird things happen to us. Some of us even have wild imaginations and can come up with the funniest things. *Tell us, I hear you saying!* Blogging has become a sensation all over the world and no we all won't hit that million just by writing an article but some of you are probably amazing at it. In fact, you might already have thousands of subscribers. If this is you, you're not capitalizing off it let me explain why.

Affiliate Marketing is performance-based marketing which a business rewards one or more affiliates (YOU) for each visitor or customer brought by the affiliate's (YOU) own marketing techniques. I'm sure by now we've seen many female celebrities promote the flat tummy tea and now you know why. Every time one of you clicked the link, they got paid well. You know you can do this as well.

You can partner with a company and earn a commission by referring your readers or anyone that visits your site. *For Example:* If you're a blogger writing about color, your brand awareness could be for Redken (affiliate marketing should be done here) or Pulprit. Deciding to write about their shades or vibrancy can draw in a new audience and some serious cash.

Being able to drive traffic to the company's website can prove difficult so you must have a clear marketing strategy with strong seo (search engine optimization) techniques to create awesome content.

<u>Vending</u>

Currently, you can buy almost everything out a vending machine.

There are over 4.5 million vending machines in the United States and sales of healthier foods are outpacing the traditional junk food vending machines by 3 times. More than half are placed strategically in office and manufacturing facilities and have even replaced cafeterias in Fortune 500 companies. Starting a successful vending business can earn 1 - 5 million dollars a year.

The same with any business is location, location, location. Making sure you have prime Real Estate is key and will be necessary if you want to maximize your profits. The structure of this type of business can be a burden when it's time to restock your machines however at a certain point you could pay someone to do it for you. Remember your time is value.

Operating a vending machine requires no special skill or training. Part time or full time, you can still produce a pocket full of change that will compound.

I've seen vending machines with hair products from hair spray to edge control in places like Beverly Hills (the Bentley of vending machines). I'm sure you can think of the different types of items you've seen like cheap stuffed animals that we never win or colorful gumballs that taste like hard air after three minutes of chewing.

This is one of my fab five and I truly love this strategy. Low start-up cost, all cash (no accounts receivable), flexible, one of a kind and scalable. It seems too easy right? I know, and it's one of the reasons why you must take it seriously. It's never easy.

YOU GOT THIS!

It's surface thinking and in developing a changed mindset, this is something you can't do. Starting a business that yields 7 billion dollars a year by simply refilling a few times a year demands your respect.

Triple Threat

Game Room, Arcade, Gaming Store

If I earned a dollar for every time I heard a story about Fortnite, Online gaming and gaming chairs, I could live a very comfortable life. Millennials love their gaming systems and so did we.

The difference today is being able to earn multiple streams of income by reselling, playing, teaching others and a bucket load of cups overflowing with gamers all over the world. This is simply known by a score or the gaming name.

Creating a talk show or podcast based on gaming, could easily land you major sponsorship if you do this successfully. Our social network is becoming more isolated with technology taking over. If you love your PlayStation the way I use to love my Xbox, maybe you should learn more about this strategy.

If online gaming isn't your thing perhaps being the proud owner of an arcade will bring out the kid in you. Maybe it's something your kid(s) say that makes you feel cool. Having the top score on your machines could win your customers a special prize beyond bragging rights (just a thought). Professional gaming is on trend to grow to 2.73 billion by year 2021 according to Statista. Over 330 million people tuned in to watch others play video games. We all have our guilty pleasures and if gaming is yours or sound like something you could be doing, you should add this to your *Topics I need to Research*.

Reselling video games and equipment can be just as profitable as a pawn shop or thrift store. With this option, it's best to use a *first come, first serve* method. You must know where the best buys are, what games are hot and where to sell them. How cool is it to have a diverse crew of stylists reading this book as female gamers? Perhaps this is where you shine because it's your guilty little pleasure and you know everything about it.

Rule of 72 - Compound Interest Made Simple

Using the Rule of 72 will tell you exactly how long it will take to double your earnings by dividing the potential interest. Example:

If you invested $5,000.00 in an investment account earning 4% interest the equation would be as follows: 72 / 4% = 18, so it will take 18 years to double money totaling 10,000.00. Small differences in your interest rates can be huge gains in earning potential. The earlier your money goes in and the longer it stays, the more you profit.

Investing at 21

4%	8%	12%	16%	Percentage
+18	+9	+6	+4.5	In Years
$5,000.00	$5,000.00	$5,000.00	$5,000.00	Amount Invested
$10,000.00	$10,000.00	$10,000.00	$10,000.00	Amount Invested

$20,000.00	$20,000.00	$20,000.00	$20,000.00	Amount Invested
$40,000.00	$40,000.00	$40,000.00	$40,000.00	Amount Invested
	$80,000.00	$80,000.00	$80,000.00	Amount Invested
		$160,000.00	$160,000.00	Amount Invested
			$320,000.00	Amount Invested
			$640,000.00	Amount Invested
			$1,280,000.00	

At a rate of 16% and patience you will arrive to millionaire status by the age of 66. It's all in the numbers. If they had taught us about this in our math class, we would all be billionaires and still be able to enjoy our life at this age. But, unfortunately, they don't.

Homework

If you are already investing or have your cash in an interest-bearing account, use the Rule of 72 and see how long you have before doubling your money. In case you don't have neither, $2/0 = 0$. Here is where you should change your mindset.

Question: If it all came down to a $1,000,000.00 today or 0.01 doubled over 30 days which will you choose?

A tale of numbers

In India, there lived a Raja who believed he was wise and fair. The people in his province were rice farmers. The Raja decreed that everyone must give nearly all their rice to him. "I will store the rice safely," the Raja promised, "so that in time of famine, everyone will have rice to eat, and no one will go hungry." Each year, the Raja's rice collectors gathered rice and carried it away to the royal storehouses.

For many years, the rice grew well. The people gave nearly all their rice to the Raja, and the storehouses were always full. But the people were left with only enough rice to get by. Then one year the rice grew badly and there was famine and hunger. The people had no rice to give to the Raja, and they had no rice to eat. The Raja's ministers implored him, "Your Highness, let us open the royal storehouses and give the rice to the people, as you promised." "No!" cried the Raja. How do I know how long the famine will last? I must have the rice for myself. A Raja must not go hungry!

Time went on, and the people grew more and more hungry. But the Raja would not give out the rice. One day, the Raja ordered a feast for himself and his court. A servant led an elephant from a royal storehouse to the palace, carrying two full baskets of rice. A village girl named Rani saw that a trickle of rice was falling from one of the baskets. Quickly she jumped up and walked along beside the elephant, catching the falling rice in her skirt. She was clever and came up with a plan.

At the palace, a guard cried, "Halt, thief! Where are you going with that rice?"

"I am not a thief," Rani replied. "This rice fell from one of the baskets, and I am returning it to the Raja."

When the Raja heard about Rani's good deed, he asked his ministers to bring her before him.

"I wish to reward you for returning what belongs to me," the Raja said to Rani. "Ask me for anything, and you shall have it."

"Your Highness," said Rani, "I do not deserve any reward at all. But if you wish, you may give me one grain of rice."

"Only one grain of rice?" exclaimed the Raja. "Surely you will allow me to reward you more plentifully, as a Raja should."

"Very well," said Rani. Today, you will give me a single grain of rice. Then, each day for thirty days you will give me double the rice you gave me the day before. Thus, tomorrow you will give me two grains of rice, the next day four grains of rice, and so on for thirty days."

"This seems to be a modest reward," said the Raja. "But you shall have it."

And Rani was presented with a single grain of rice.

The next day, Rani was presented with 2 grains of rice.

And the following day, Rani was presented with 4 grains of rice.

On the ninth day, Rani was presented with 256 grains of rice. She had received in all five hundred and eleven grains of rice, enough for only a small handful. "This girl is honest, but not very clever," thought the Raja. "She would have gained more rice by keeping what fell into her skirt!"

On the twelfth day, Rani received 2048 grains of rice, about four handfuls.

On the thirteenth day, she received 4096 grains of rice, enough to fill a bowl.

On the sixteenth day, Rani was presented with a bag containing 32,768 grains of rice. All together she had enough rice for two bags. "This doubling up adds up to more rice than I expected" thought the Raja. "But surely her reward won't amount to much more."

On the twenty-first day, she received 1,048,576 grains of rice, enough to fill a basket.

On the twenty-fourth day, Rani was presented with 8,388,608 grains of rice–enough to fill eight baskets, which were carried to her by eight royal deer.

On the twenty-seventh day, thirty-two brahma bulls were needed to deliver sixty-four baskets of rice. The raja was deeply troubled. "One grain of rice has grown very great indeed," he thought. "But I shall fulfill the reward to the end, as a raja should."

On the twenty-ninth day, Rani was presented with the contents of two royal storehouses.

On the thirtieth and final day, two hundred and fifty-six elephants crossed the province, carrying the contents of the last four royal storehouses- 536,870,912 grains of rice.

Altogether, Rani had received more than **one billion grains of rice**. The raja had no more rice to give. "And what will you do with this rice," said the raja with a sigh, "now that I have none?"

"I shall give it to all the hungry people," said Rani, "and I shall leave a basket of rice for you, too, if you promise from now on to take only as much rice as you need."

"I promise," said the Raja. And for the rest of his days, the Raja was truly wise and fair, as a Raja should be. If only our government could understand the power in this wise tale, the world would know very little suffering.

This is the true power of compound interest and why having true patience with your money allows it to bloom just the same as a tree planted in the ground or growth of a human being from the time of conception. Imagine saving money from your child's first birthday and Christmas cards over 18 years old now. How much more could that be if you had invested it?

Watch what happens to this penny over thirty days!

Day 1	$.01	Day 16	$327.68
Day 2	$.02	Day 17	$655.36
Day 3	$.04	Day 18	$1,310.72
Day 4	$.08	Day 19	$2,621.44
Day 5	$.16	Day 20	$5,242.88
Day 6	$.32	Day 21	$10,485.76
Day 7	$.64	Day 22	$20,971.52
Day 8	$1.28	Day 23	$41,943.04
Day 9	$2.56	Day 24	$83,886.08
Day 10	$5.12	Day 25	$167,772.16
Day 11	$10.24	Day 26	$335,544.32
Day 12	$20.48	Day 27	$671,088.64
Day 13	$40.96	Day 28	$1,342,177.28
Day 14	$81.92	Day 29	$2,684,354.56
Day 15	$163.84	Day 30	$5,368,709.12

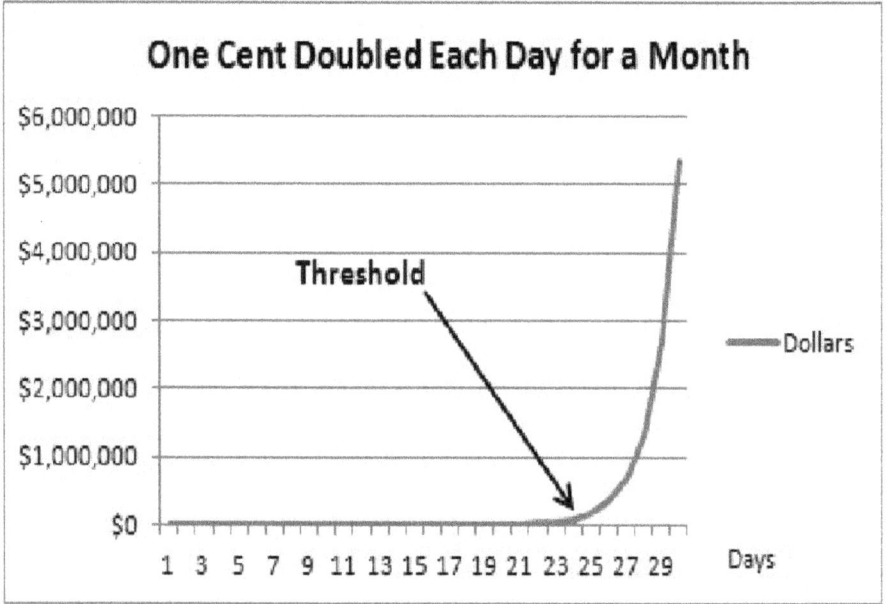

One Cent Doubled Each Day for a Month

Threshold

Dollars

Days

CHAPTER 10

UNDERSTANDING YOUR WEALTH POTENTIAL

Generational Wealth

We not only do what we love just to make our clients look good, but we also like to make money and lots of it. We need this money to take care of our family and loved ones but what happens when your back gives out, you develop arthritis in your hand what is your plan b? Have you built enough wealth to generate income for your family for decades yet to come? Are you building a legacy your Mom and/or kids can be proud of? We put huge strains on our bodies, and I think it's time we have something to show for it and material things just won't cut it.

5% of the planet has generational wealth

15% of the planet is considered middle class

80% of the planet will have to work past the retirement age or live off a subsidized income. This disheartening percentage is why I chose to educate myself about money instead of hair. Hair stylist are working longer hours and years of retirement seem to never come. The lifestyle you've been brainwashed to live is keeping you behind the eight ball, you must shift the paradigm.

Think about the legacy you want to leave behind and how you're tired of living paycheck to paycheck or client to client. If you really want to enjoy the fruits of your labor learn to have patience. I know it is extremely hard because it's in our nature to want it now. Instead try focusing on the journey you will take to reach your end game.

"Riches may not bring happiness but neither does poverty". -Sophia Irene Loeb

"The real source of wealth and capital in this new era is not in material things. It is the human mind, the human spirit, the human imagination and our faith in the future." Steve Forbes, Billionaire, Publisher

"A man's mind stretched to a new idea never goes back to its original dimensions." Oliver Wendell Hohmes

"Success is on the razor edge of failure." Jon Stallings

Franchise

Investing in a business that already has a system in place allows you to enter an industry that knows exactly who their target audience is and the most effective way to connect. The most difficult challenge as with any business can be location and capital. Some franchises expect the funds to be liquid (cash) not to include your startup cost.

"Franchisees are often referred to as formula entrepreneurs", says Michael Seid, managing director of MSA Worldwide and author of *Franchising for Dummies*.

"An entrepreneur is quite independent and typically creates their own method through madness, while a formula entrepreneur has more of a desire to invest in guaranteed methods and systems, they can execute without significant changes.

Costs involved with a franchise can be steep. The initial franchise fee could range from $15,000.00 to $50,000.00, and in some cases, it doesn't include your cost for training. In the United States, the franchise fee for Subway is $15,000.00, but the total investment to open a Subway restaurant can range between $116,000.00 and $263,000.00."

https://money.usnews.com/

Goals

- To enjoy life, increase your income by at least 10% a year
- Save more than you saved the previous year
- Increase the percentage of what you saved the previous year. Instead of saving 10%, save 15%, 20% or more
- If you make more than 200,000 save a minimum of 25%

When you have reached an income of one million, it's mandatory to save 35%. **YOUR LEGACY DEPENDS ON IT!**

Write down your goals

Be Specific (Crystal Clear)

S – Specific (What do you want)

M – Measurable (How do you plan to get there)

A – Actionable (What steps can you take to achieve it)

R – Realistic (Be rational and logical)

T – Time Base (Have a time frame)

Passive Income Ideas

1. Although having your own product line and restaurant are considered passive income, I choose not to discuss strategy. The truth is the capital needed and knowledge is a lot more complex. Both strategies require you to be familiar across an array of industries.

2. Strategy isn't a trick. It is a tool. Start to strategize about your business the same way you do when it comes to getting and having what you want. Plan to pay for courses from people whose names or brands you use, work with or train with. There is very little gained from learning a technique besides a new skill. The fact is if you don't know how to capitalize on the skills you already possess, how will adding another one help?

How will new clients hear of you? How will you promote or market to your target audience? Who is your target audience?

It's not just your skills that's keeping your business stagnant. It's your marketing strategies or lack of. Rumor has it, it's 80% marketing and 20% skill. Truly we've all seen the mediocre stylist that stays booked. The difference is a marketing strategy. They find ways to connect with their customers.

Limits

"Running a business is simple, not easy. you must push yourself beyond your predetermined limit." -Mel Robbins CNN Commentator, . Author

Limit (n) – A point or level beyond which something does not or may not extend or pass. "the **limits of** presidential power"

(v) set or serve as a limit to

"try to limit the amount you drink"

Simply put, when you think of the word limit who sets it? You or someone else? In this case, decide to have NO LIMITS!

There is nothing more satisfying than making it on your own terms. YOU ARE SELF MADE!

Everything you are has come to you from your actions. Now take BIGGER ACTIONS, EPIC ACTIONS! Push yourself beyond previous limitations. Be FEARLESS! The world is your playground, and you only get one shot to make it count. Believe in yourself. You can do it. NO LIMITS, NO BOUNDARIES, NO DOUBTS. Respect is not given it's earned. I don't need an alarm clock. My goals WAKE ME! My desires WAKE ME! My purpose WAKE ME!

Sacrifice now, Enjoy later. Push hard now, Relax later. UNLEASH THE BEAST!

I have my own heart! I have my own dreams!

- COWARDS never start
- THE Weak never finish
- THE Strong never quit
- MAKE IT HAPPEN!
- REPEAT DAILY!

Check out the entire speech here!
https://www.youtube.com/watch?v=Ig7INVS6wEl

"When you have a dream, you have to dream globally but win locally". Jack Ma- United Nations Entrepreneur Seminar

Writing this book has been my pleasure! I appreciate each one of you who has taken the time to invest in themselves and the importance of establishing financial freedom. Over the years I have researched and learned so much that I want you to have these tools as well. Here, I have compiled a list of some of my most helpful tools through the links below along with helpful tools to help you along your journey.

Business Credit

The only way to build business credit is through tradelines and I can't stress enough how you should never link your social security number.

The perception, lenders, vendors and creditors have of your business is critical to your ability to build strong business credit. There are over 15 credibility points that are necessary to have a strong foundation and as a bonus, I'm submitting there here:

1. Use your exact business legal name
2. Include any recorded DBA filing you will use (fictitious, trade name or assumed name. You could face penalties if you chose not to comply.

3. Ensure your business name is the same on your corporation papers, licenses and bank statements.
4. Corporate Entities are the members of your corporation
5. LLC (Limited Liability Corp, S Corp or Corporation
6. Must have an EIN
7. Must have a 411 Listing
8. Confirm all agencies, banks and creditors have your business listed with the same tax ID.
9. Use a Business Address (not your house). Can't be home based address
10. No PO BOX
11. Need a fax number
12. Must have a website
13. Company e-mail
14. The date on your bank account is considered your start date for lenders
15. Don't ever use free email (buy your domain)
16. Lenders perceive 1800 numbers or toll-free numbers a sign of credibility
17. No UPS addresses

D-U-N-S Number or DUNS & Bradstreet

Your DUNS number plays an important role in enabling your business to borrow without a personal guarantee. It also helps to obtain vendor accounts.

A vendor line of credit is when a company extends a line of credit to your business on "Net" 15,30,60 or 90-day terms. This means you can purchase their products or services up to a maximum dollar amount.

Even if asked, NEVER give your social security number

When your first net 30 account reports to DUNS & Bradstreet (D&B), the automated system will activate your file along with Experian and Equifax.

Some vendors require an initial prepaid order.

Vendors don't need to serve 100% of your business needs. You want the tradelines.

Most merchants and some retailers offer business credit they just choose not to advertise. Build up your tradelines to receive revolving credit options. Some vendors won't approve you unless you have established some trade lines.

After 5 tradelines are secured with vending accounts, you can apply for revolving accounts that are paid monthly instead of paying the entire balance in full. Most stores won't approve a business owner unless they have an established profile and score. Try to obtain at least10 Revolving accounts before you apply for credit cards.

This strategy is one of many, however, if you want to build your credit profile, have your stuff together or expect to be denied. Your goal is to submit a complete application that will get you past the initial screening process and on to the next step. Think of the screening process as one that is designed to kick you out if any of the information is incorrect.

Tradelines	Revolving Credit
Quill.com	Office Depot
Uline Shipping Supplies	Staples
Reliable Office Supplies	Amazon

pdf for business credit

https://www.govassociation.org/resources/Documents/how%20to%20build%20business%20credit%20060518.pdf

Email Automation through Contant
Contactconstant-contact.evyy.net/vgLZA

Going digital is time consuming and costly. It would benefit your business to work with a reputable company that offers consistent support and a free trial with no credit card required.

Joining The Chamber of Commerce

https://frankjkenny.com/join-local-chamber-commerce/

Specialization is the shortest way to the top in our industry. Become the best at the things or thing you are growing and selling.

What is SCORE?

SCORE is the nation's largest network of volunteer, expert business mentors, with more than 10,000 Volunteers in 300 Chapters.

As a resource partner of the U.S. Small Business Administration (SBA), SCORE has helped more than 11 million entrepreneurs through mentoring, workshops and educational resources since 1964.

With SCORE, you are not alone on your business journey. Visit www.score.org for more information.

Any questions you have about business can be answered through this program. It is an optimal tool that will assist you with excelling in your business and cut down on trial and error.

Writing a book? Tell the world your story or create one. Knowledge and testimonials are meant to be shared. We learn and grow from one another. You never know who you can inspire by your words. My journey to write this book was a way to empower many souls at the same time while creating content to stand the test of time. What valuable information can the world learn from you? How can your story make an impact on one person's life? Well, you won't know until you take that leap. You must release that energy while unleashing your light. Progress doesn't happen by wishful thinking. It happens by action. Taking action is the best decision you will ever make to get you to your destination.

One thing I'd like to leave you with is remembering that this is just the beginning of your journey from behind the chair to earning 7 figures. Embrace it! Own it! Enjoy it!

Affirmations to help you with embracing a new mindset.

1. With change comes change
2. Make the money. Don't let the money make you
3. It's time to go after what I want
4. I will become a shear millionaire
5. I have no limits
6. I am whatever I want to be
7. I choose to chase my financial freedom
8. Creating wealth affords me the life I want to leave for my children
9. I am on my way to earning a 7-figure income
10. Nothing will keep me from my dream, my happiness and my money

Interested in holding an in-depth class at your salon, joining our **Mentorship Program** or becoming a part of the team? Feel free to contact me via e-mail and become part of The Millionaire Guide for Hair and Beauty Salons Book Tour.

Email @ ninaskye@hairchroniclesstudio.com

Follow Me on IG and Facebook @ hairchroniclesstudio
To learn all things hair and business.

You can also follow me on Twitter for updates, random specials and trending updates @hairchronstudio

This Book Series is just the beginning as the economy and business is ever changing. Please use hashtags #ShearMillionaire & #EdgyRockerRebellious

References from Quotes & Chapter Information

Know Thyself:
https://www.forbes.com/sites/jeffkauflin/2017/05/10/only-15-of-people-are-self-aware-heres-how-to-change/#7c5526652b8c

Failure:
https://www.politifact.com/truth-o-meter/statements/2015/apr/13/rick-santorum/90-american-workers-dont-own-their-own-business-ri/

Are You a Leader:
https://money.usnews.com/money/blogs/on-retirement/articles/7-myths-about-millionaires

Flipping vs Renting:
https://fitsmallbusiness.com/taxes-on-flipping-houses/

Cannabis:
https://www.forbes.com/sites/debraborchardt/2017/01/03/marijuana-sales-totaled-6-7-billion-in-2016/#2311c07775e3

https://www.puffpuffpost.com/cannabis-market-predicted-to-hit-146-billion-by-2025/

https://www.statista.com/statistics/748044/number-video-gamers-world/